*Life's Joy Killers
and Joy Makers*

Life's Joy Killers and *Joy Makers*

God's Way of Bringing and Keeping Joy in Your Life

LaVon Koerner

RESOURCE *Publications* • Eugene, Oregon

LIFE'S JOY KILLERS AND JOY MAKERS
God's Way of Bringing and Keeping Joy in Your Life

Copyright © 2020 LaVon Koerner. All rights reserved. Except for brief quotations in critical publications or reviews, no part of this book may be reproduced in any manner without prior written permission from the publisher. Write: Permissions, Wipf and Stock Publishers, 199 W. 8th Ave., Suite 3, Eugene, OR 97401.

Resource Publications
An Imprint of Wipf and Stock Publishers
199 W. 8th Ave., Suite 3
Eugene, OR 97401

www.wipfandstock.com

PAPERBACK ISBN: 978-1-7252-8055-7
HARDCOVER ISBN: 978-1-7252-8056-4
EBOOK ISBN: 978-1-7252-8057-1

Manufactured in the U.S.A. 09/04/20

Scripture quotations marked ESV are from the Holy Bible, English Standard Version®, copyright © 2001 by Crossway, a publishing ministry of Good News Publishers. All rights reserved. ESV Text Edition: 2016

Scripture quotations marked KJV are from the King James Version. Public Domain

Scripture quotations marked NIV are from the New International Version®, NIV®. Copyright © 1973, 1978, 1984, 2011 by Biblica.

Scripture quotations marked TLB are from the Living Bible, copyright © 1971 by Tyndale House.

Scripture quotations marked NASB are from the New American Standard Bible, copyright © 1960, 1962, 1963, 1968, 1971, 1972, 1973, 1975, 1977,1995 by the Lockman Foundation.

Scripture quotations marked NKJV are from the New King Janes Version®. Copyright © 1982 by Thomas Nelson, Inc.

Scripture quotations marked NLT are from the New Living Translation, copyright © 1986, 2004, 2015, Tyndale House Foundation

Scripture quotations marked MSG are from The Message, copyright 2002, Eugene H. Peterson

Scripture quotations marked CSB are from the Christian Standard Bible, Copyright 2016, 2020, B&H Publishing Group.

Scripture quotations marked EHV are from the Evangelical Heritage Version. Copyright Northwestern Publishing House.

Scripture quotations marked DARBY are from the John Nelson Darby translation of the New Testament in 1887 with revised editions in 1872 and 1884.

Scripture quotations marked AMP are from the Amplified Bible. Copyright 1954, 1958, 1962, 1964, 1965, 1987, 2015, Zondervan Publishing House

Scripture quotations marked ESVUK are from the English Standard Version Anglicized. Copyright date not specified. Good News Publishers

Are You the Person to Whom This Book Is Dedicated?

I had a specific person in mind when I wrote this book. If it was you, then you filled my heart with empathic concern coupled with tons of compassion. Often, during the months of writing, I stopped to pray for you knowing the joy for your daily personal journey through life could be in great peril. My heart ached to be with you to discuss these things. More than once, I had tears in my eyes as I typed the words of these personal messages while thinking about you. I could feel the hurt from which you are being subjected in this crazy world gone mad. I so wanted to hug you and tell you that you are not alone, that you are greatly loved, and that there is a way for you to be alright and filled with a steady and enduring joyfulness.

If you are that person, allow me to whisper even now into your ear as you read this book, and tell you how I know that you can and will be okay. But first, are you that person to whom I'm writing? If you answer any of these questions with a yes, then indeed you are that very person to whom this book is dedicated.

Do you sometimes wonder if God is mindful of you and your personal predicaments and is willing to do something about them in your behalf?

Do you wish for calmer reactions by having a quiet and sufficient strength to navigate brutal, unjust, and unfair situations to which you are often subjected?

Do you ever wish that you could feel more love for more people, more often?

Do you ever feel too small, helpless, and intimated in a world with so many big problems?

Do you ever wish you had better answers than you now have for life's perplexing questions?

As you journey through life, do you sometimes get frightened by your future or where you may be headed?

Do you ever feel all alone and not understood?

Do you ever yearn for a better, more consistent, and more personal one-on-one relationship with God?

Have you ever wished that you had been born smarter, wiser, better looking, and/or more talented?

If you said yes to some or many of these questions, then you are the very person I had in my mind, in my prayers, and in my heart when I wrote this book. And I can't wait to meet you in heaven because you and I are an awful lot alike. We must take some time in eternity to swap stories!

LaVon

Additional materials supporting LaVon's book, Life's Joy Killers and Joy Makers along with his first book, Untangling the Seven Desires of Your Heart can be found and obtained by visiting his website at:

lavoninspirations.org

Contents

Preface | ix
Introduction | xi
Chapter Introduction | 1

1. **GETTING GOD'S BIG PICTURE RIGHT | 3**

   Part A: Journey Joy Killer One | 4
   You Are Being Stalked by a Murderer

   Part B: Journey Joy Maker One | 9
   Being Sure!

2. **GOD'S WAY OF HAVING A BOLD SELF-CONFIDENCE | 15**

   Part A: Journey Joy Killer Two | 17
   Escaping Shame

   Part B: Journey Joy Maker Two | 27
   Defining a Roadmap for Your Life Journey

3. **DEFYING SIN'S GRAVITATIONAL PULL DOWNWARD | 34**

   Part A: Journey Joy Killer Three | 36
   The Three Slippery Steps Descending Down

   Part B: Journey Joy Maker Three | 44
   Getting Near to God

4. **RETHINKING YOUR RESPONSE TO SIN | 51**

   Part A: Journey Joy Killer Four | 52
   Do You Have a Sinful View of Sin?

   Part B: Journey Joy Maker Four | 60
   Are You Being Pushed or Pulled into Your Days?

5. Allowing God's Love to Determine Your Self-Esteem | 66

Part A: Journey Joy Killer Five | 67
Is Your Self-Identity Slowly Killing You?

Part B: Journey Joy Maker Five | 80
Are You Benefiting from Both Revelations?

6. Understanding God's Way of Managing the People in Your Life | 89

Part A: Journey Joy Killer Six | 90
The People Pleasing Prison

Part B: Journey Joy Maker Six | 99
Are You Love Ready?

7. Extracting Anxiety from Your Life | 111

Part A: Journey Joy Killer Seven | 112
Worry Defeated

Part B: Journey Joy Maker Seven | 123
Living Behind God's Line of Protection

8. Winning the Final Battle for Your Soul before It's Fought | 130

Part A: Journey Joy Killer Eight | 131
Knowing and Defeating Satan's Strategy

Part B: Journey Joy Maker Eight | 138
Managing the Crossover Effect

One Final but Essential Thought | 147
Epilogue: How and Why This Book Happened | 150

Preface

I'M OFTEN ASKED, "WHY did you write a book about joy and not happiness?" My short answer is because joy is so much more beautiful and meaningful than is happiness. Sheryl Crow, an American musician, famously wrote in a song, "If it makes you happy, it can't be that bad. If it makes you happy, then why the hell are you so sad?" Crow apparently could discern that being happy isn't always what is best for us.

That is because happiness is viewed as an emotion in which we experience feelings ranging from contentment and satisfaction to bliss and intense pleasure, whereas joy is deeper and stronger, less common feeling than happiness. But Joy is much more than just an emotion. It is a "state of mind." We experience joy when we achieve selflessness to the point of personal sacrifice. We feel joy when we are spiritually connected to God and are in the process of being used by him.

In biblical times, I believe that the words *joy*, and *happiness* were on occasion, interchangeable. But in todays' modern language norms, the two words have come to have different meanings and implications. Allow this chart to reflect and summarize the common differences in today's language patterns:

Happiness Versus Joyfulness

Happiness	Joyfulness
Is triggered by external stimulating situations	Is triggered by internal successes and achievements
Is seen as more temporary (comes and goes)	Is seen as more stable and enduring

Preface

Happiness Versus Joyfulness

Happiness	Joyfulness
Is more superficial and interim	Is deeper and stronger and persists longer
Is generated through emotions and feelings	Is generated through fulfillment and meaningfulness
Is created by your natural reactions	Is created by your spiritual involvements
Is anchored in your moods	Is anchored in your soul

Perhaps the very best way to see these differences on display can be found in Christ's temperament as he was heading straight towards his awful crucifixion. Here is how the writer of Hebrews noted his most unusual and surprising attribute and recorded it for our encouragement and edification:

> *Let us fix our eyes on Jesus, the author and perfecter of our faith, who for the joy set before him endured the cross.* (Heb 12:2a, NASB)

This is an amazing observation of Jesus. You wouldn't say Jesus was happy to be nailed and hung on the cross in pain, agony and humiliation. But it does make sense that when you contemplate his massive love for each of us, it became his joy to die for us while envisioning in real time, our joy in the very salvation he was providing at that very minute on calvary's cross. Hence the Biblical word descriptor of *"joy"* applied to him, even under those gruesome conditions. At that precise moment, our salvation joy became His joy. This shows that more than anything in the world, our involvement in the work and love of Christ by bringing joy to others can and will produce an unmatchable and soul-felt joy unequaled by any happiness available in or from this world. And "yes," you can be joyful and in an unhappy situation at the very same time. Jesus proved it, and because of him, each of us can experience it as well. When we know all is well, regardless of what is going on in our lives, we will have joy. And that is why this book focuses on God's way of bringing and keeping God's abundance of joy in your life!

Introduction

The Bible's Counterintuitive Approach for Living Your Life Journey

WE ARE ALL ON a journey from birth to death and beyond. Our world instructs us to do everything possible to live long as we can, and in the process, we are constantly being seduced into dreaming of retiring in the lap of luxury with no cares and worries in the world. We are told, "You only get to live once, so live large. Travel and see all you can see and do all you can do. Then die with no regrets." But is this God's advice?

Each of us has different talents and have been born in different places with different challenges and different advantages. And on top of all of that, we each make different choices in line with our different passions. As a result of all these differences, it isn't any wonder that in our older years we will all end up in very different situations for a host of different reasons. I don't think there is one size of life-ending goal that fits all. Nor is it wise to set unrealistic expectations that may or may not be in accordance with God's will for our lives.

But with that being said, the Bible gives a very different goal as to how and why to journey through life, which is the subject of this book. And it should be no surprise that God's ways are not our ways. To get us off and running on our individual life journeys, let's start with embracing God's goal of how to end up in life. God wants us to accomplish a joyful journey by getting younger, not older. The goal in life is not dying old but living long enough to die young. That's very counterintuitive, and it's not an option and it is not up for grabs or debate, it's a command! Jesus stated it this way:

> ..."*Suffer little children, and forbid them not, to come unto me: for of such is the kingdom of heaven.* (Matt 19:14, KJV)

Introduction

"Verily I say unto you, whosoever shall not receive the kingdom of God as a little child, he shall not enter therein." (Mark 10:15, KJV)

I know you recognize these verses and have probably heard or read them a hundred times. But have you ever seen and thought about those very strict last five words at the end? That's some strong language coming straight from the mouth of our Lord Jesus when he emphatically says,

"He shall not enter therein."

Take note of what he said and ponder what he clearly means. Without mincing any words, we will not be allowed to enter heaven as old, worn out, bitter, and cantankerous grumps. We will only be allowed to enter heaven like fresh enthusiastic children filled with a cheerful wide-eyed fascination of life, with our minds filled with the spirit of wonder and our exuberant hearts eager to explore and be in love with being loved by God. He is talking about innocence, not childishness, not bitterness, but eagerness to see and experience an all-powerful God, not callused and numb or blinded to all the beauty of God's love that daily surrounds us. He wants us to come to the end of life and die by sliding into home plate in a cloud of dust—and immediately standing up while dusting ourselves off asking God, "What's next?" To reach this commanded childhood state of optimistic youthfulness, we can't be carrying any accumulated and unforgiven baggage. We can't have become old cynical skeptics, no matter how hard life has been or is currently being on us. We can't have stopped dreaming of how God can use us. If or when we stop dreaming, we instantly give our physical bodies permission to begin the dying process. God's personal calling on our lives does not come with an expiration date.

We can't become so preoccupied with being safe that we stop taking chances in our forever endeavor to serve and glorify him by loving the loveless. And like a child, our guard needs to have come down and we still must be hurtable, vulnerable, and defenseless. He is not asking us to be stupid, but unafraid to boldly love and be loved. Life must never stop being an adventure for us. We simply must become and stay childlike in our zestful approach to living.

This book was written to assist you in becoming a joyful and excited kid the older you get. It will tell you about eight journey joy killers that will need to be removed and corrected and it will identify eight journey joy makers to put in their place. Each chapter in this book will inch you

Introduction

back into that joyful, playful childhood disposition that Jesus finds so very attractive and endearing.

As Jesus again said,

> "Verily I say unto you, except ye be converted, and become as little children, ye shall not enter into the kingdom of heaven." (Matt 18:3, KJV)

Just as children have learned safety in the presence of their parents, we must become filled with the certainty of faith of being totally safe with our heavenly father's provision on a day-by-day basis. At some point we will have either become self-protective, or we will have become totally secure in God's protection. Either we are very busy digging out a living, desperate to make or keep our own selves happy, or we will have discovered a Holy Spirit led and joy filled life and we will have become completely satisfied in Jesus, knowing he is all we need. Heads up, there is no in between!

This book is not about finishing your journey and ending up old, but it is about becoming younger by the day. You are never too old to get younger! And the closer you get to Jesus, the younger you will feel, and your excitement will grow each day as you pitch your tent one day closer to eternity.

Chapter Introduction

FIRST, A QUICK WORD on how and why this book has been designed the way that it is. You will find that the book is intended to follow the pattern in the Scripture where we are told to *"Put to death therefore what is earthly in you"* (Col. 3:5), then a few verses later we are instructed to *"put on the new self."* (Col. 3:10). This "Taking Off" and "Putting On" are called, "Journey Joy Killers" and "Journey Joy Makers" in this book. And as you read about each Joy Killer and each Joy Maker, remember that God never asks you to "put something down," unless He has "something better for you to pick up."

Each **Joy Killer** is targeting an area where some adjustment in your thinking needs to be made if we want to experience more Joy in our life's Journey. Often, it is not a common "Sin of Commission," but rather an uncommon "Sin of Omission." It may be that you have unconsciously adopted the world's way of thinking that needs to be corrected. Or your thinking may be incomplete, or maybe you have never thought about it at all. And you may be surprised to find that some of these false thinking patterns and false philosophies are very popular, even in our churches. The correction starts where the Bible advocates that it should, "Be transformed by the renewing of your mind." (Romans 12:2) You will find yourself being challenged to think differently about some very specific areas in your daily life. I pray that you enjoy the opportunity to look at some things in a very different light. I think that is why we all read books. Right?

By contrast, each **Joy Maker** will focus on something new that you should consider adding into your life. Again, it will follow the same Biblical formula where you can adopt some new way to think about how you are living. This will entail some prayerful decision making on your part. It would necessitate the adoption of new ways to see life differently which would result in doing some things you may have never done before. But in each case, the end result is always the same—more Joy.

Life's Joy Killers and Joy Makers

Each section in the book will be closed with a poem that will enable you to have some time to mediate and ponder on some of the key principles you've just learned. Meditation of this type will solidify those new concepts that may have just been implanted into your thinking. The poems are designed to emotionally move that which you've just discovered from your head into your heart. Take a few minutes to review the poem, most people find it Spiritually illuminating as to what God wants you to learn and feel from what you've just studied.

Also, after each Part A and Part B in each chapter, there is a place provided for you to "Journal" your thoughts before moving on to the next section. If you have never journaled before, you may notice by the time you finish this book that you've picked up a new habit. Personal reflection is healthy, especially when it is coupled with God's truths. It is surprising how just making a few notes brings clarity as to what God is saying to you and some things that God may want you to take out of your life or put into your life. Enjoy!

1

Getting God's Big Picture Right

It is impossible to have or keep an accurate perspective from what is happening to you every day if you do not have an accurate "Big Picture" in your mind to which to compare it. At the end of Chapter one, it is my prayer that you will have a better and more accurate "big picture" in your mind. The Joy Killer (Part A) in this chapter tells it like it is and therefore, it has some uncomfortable and ugly concepts in it. But our journey needs to be anchored in the reality of what we are up against. My prayer is that it will not discourage you but embolden you to tackle some difficult challenges of daily life utilizing the power of Jesus to win joyful victory after victory.

The Joy Maker (Part B) in this chapter deals with a foundational view of why we, as Christians, can feel so secure in what we believe and If you have some doubts, this may be a good time to address them. God's wants you to go to bed every night secure in your relationship with Him knowing He has you covered! The future chapters will focus on "advanced" topics that will necessitate that you have a solid foundation for your faith upon which to build.

These two parts (Joy Killer and Joy Maker) of this chapter are intended to make you absolutely sure of your relationship with Jesus, and that you do not need to wake up in the middle of the night wondering where you stand with God.

Enjoy Chapter 1, It will give you the foundation needed for being able to apply the new spiritual concepts that you will be provided in the rest of the book.

In His loving and mighty grip,

LaVon

Part A
Journey Joy Killer One

You Are Being Stalked by a Murderer

The Ugly Truth about Your Life's Death-Defying Journey

THIS IS THE WORST chapter in the book for you to have to read and I'm sorry about it coming first. I hesitated in writing it because it's filled with so many awful concepts. But how could I write about your journey from your conception to your death and beyond without documenting the causer of your eventual death, the killer of all killers—joy killer 1?

You will never fully love or yearn for life in heaven until you first understand its alternative. Nor will you ever love or appreciate what Christ did for you until you see the danger you are or were in and how he intervened to offer you the ultimate escape. To do that, I need to share some very alarming and unpleasant truths. Brace yourself but read on!

> *You are of your father the devil, and your will is to do your father's desires. He was a murderer from the beginning, and does not stand in the truth, because there is no truth in him. When he lies, he speaks out of his own character, for he is a liar and the father of lies.* (John 8:44, ESV)

That one verse summarizes the supreme intent of Satan, and it is to put to death every person. Said in a more personal way, his purpose, as far as you are concerned, is to murder you or get you murdered, causing you to die and stay dead for all eternity in deadly torment. Satan's concept of death is simply being separated from God and his love. And according to this verse, he will do it through lies whereby he deceives you about both

Part A: Journey Joy Killer One

life and death. His first recorded lie to Adam and Eve was, *"You shall not surely die,"*(Gen 3:4, ESV) which was a direct contradiction to God's command to *"not eat of the tree of life because you shall surely die"*. When they bought into that lie and ate of the fruit from the tree of life, death entered the human race.

> *Therefore, just as sin came into the world through one man, and death through sin, and so death spread to all men because all sinned.* (Rom 5:12, ESV)

We are doomed to die, but it is much worse than that. He wants to kill all our hope, our enthusiasm of living, our belief in the existence of God's life-supporting love, the thrill of companionship with God, and the security of being irrevocably coupled with God by being in his forever royal family. We must resist the temptation to soften the terrible news of death by not being duped into thinking that death is the natural end of life. There is absolutely nothing natural about death. God created life, your life. And more than that, your life was never to end. He (God) personalized your life in every aspect at the point of conception in your mother's womb. Read it for yourself in Psalm 139 and be blown away by what he says about you. Begin with verse 13 where David is talking to God about how he (David) came into being:

> *For you formed my inward parts; you knitted me together in my mother's womb I praise you, for I am fearfully and wonderfully made. Wonderful are your works; my soul knows it very well. My frame was not hidden from you, when I was being made in secret, intricately woven in the depths of the earth. Your eyes saw my unformed substance in your book were written, every one of them, the days that were formed for me, when as yet there was none of them. How precious to me are Your thoughts, O God! How vast is the sum of them!* (Ps 139:13–17, ESV)

You just cannot read that and not feel loved by the huge amount of personal attention and involvement God invests into each of us during that miracle of life in our mother's womb. This is exactly why the price tag on life is so very high and why Jesus had no alternative but to sacrifice his life for our precious lives. Jesus had no choice but to die in order to reverse the murderous intentions of Satan to eternally destroy us through death, eternal death.

Please note that in God's creation process of you, he did not delegate or assign this to an angel, he is personally involved in every person's conceptional design in their mother's womb. And it is not just our own individual fingerprints that are different, its everything about us that makes us 100 percent unique. There is only one copy of you; his copyright on you signifies that he made you and that he personally wants to have deep and personal relationship with you for all eternity. He could not be prouder of you and your potential to influence this world in a positive way! And on top of that, his heart yearns to be connected to your heart. Satan's murderous intentions are to disconnect you from God through death.

If you get these foundational truths, only then can you begin to understand the depth of Satan's hatred of both God and you. He uses you to get at God. To hurt you is to hurt God, to destroy you, is to destroy God's masterpiece, and to murder you before you are saved by Christ is to deny God from being able to have a glorious relationship with you for all eternity. Your unpreventable death is Satan's final effort to disconnect you from God. But, because of Jesus and his resurrection power, you can be snatched out of the jaws of death to finish the plan God had for you when you were created in your mother's womb. He made you for himself. Get this, you are so very important to Satan's murder scheme because you are so very important to God's love scheme. Therefore, you must

> *Be sober-minded; be watchful. Your adversary the devil prowls around like a roaring lion, seeking someone to devour. Resist him, firm in your faith.* (1 Pet 5:8–9a, ESV)

How Satan accomplishes your murder can take any number of methods, but the goal is always the same, he wants you dead, period, and disconnected from God and his forever love of you. He may use a doctor to dismember you in your mother's womb or have a Hitler transport you to a concentration camp where you will be gassed to death, or maybe you will be gunned down in a Chicago street gang war. He may even tempt you to kill yourself or get you to blindly commit death on the installment plan by doing drugs, drinking, or just eating wrongly. How he does it is not so important. He is 100 percent committed to your murder because he must take you out of God's plan to have a loving relationship with you for ever and ever and to use you to his glory while on planet earth! Satan must keep you from God's infectious satisfying love aimed at you.

Don't you see that? Once you conclude that, you will then be ready to get serious about your journeying through life God's way! And in the end, you will finally escape the clutches of death and pass on to eternal life with the one who loves you most by defying the one who hates you most!

Part A: Journey Joy Killer One

I'm Wanted Dead

I don't like this subject, so I avoid thinking or talking about it.
It depresses me, so I just bury it into my subconscious, I admit.

To know that Satan, with his army of minions, wants me dead,
takes my breath away and leaves me both numb and helplessly sad.

On my own, and knowing all my own weaknesses, I feel both defenseless and helpless,
fighting against my evil heart, our evil world, and the evil one, leaves me hopeless.

Without hearing the good news informing me about Jesus who wants to rescue me,
I hesitate to even think about the mess of trouble in which I would be.

Destined to be Satan's victim with a sad, meaningless, and scarred life.
Besieged by relationship conflicts, causing torment and unending strife.

But hearing about Jesus, who used love to fix my broken heart,
Showing me new ways of living by His Spirit empowering me with a new start.

Admitting all my failures and seeing the ugly world of hurt in which I live,
I was hopelessly trapped, unable to get free, no matter how much effort I could give.

Then Jesus loved me with a love that I never knew existed,
He encircled me with a tough love that made me feel protected.

It changed everything, life took on a new joy and a radiant meaning,
His forgiveness removed all the gunk and grime with a complete soul cleaning.

Not only this, but now I am "Wanted Alive,"
and I'm a witness that on life's journey, one can survive.

Getting God's Big Picture Right

My Journal for My Journey

When I think about Satan's hatred of me I . . .

When I think about God's personal involvement in my creation in my mother's womb, I feel . . .

I'm committed to defying Satan's plan for my life by . . .

The first thing I'm going to do to resist Satan's Joy-killing hatred is . . .

Part B

Journey Joy Maker One

Being Sure!

A Contented and Joyful Backseat Rider

It seems like it was just yesterday. We finished chores early and I let the cows back out into the pasture after they had been milked. It was a pleasant June summer night. Dad loaded us in the '53 red Dodge car and we headed to town where the traveling circus had arrived for their three-day summer visit.

I should have been ecstatic; I had never seen a clown or a live elephant, or people swinging on a high trapeze under the big tent. For an 11-year-old, rural, backwoods farm boy, this is the kind of night that only comes along once in a lifetime. All the kids at school were talking about it. My brother couldn't keep from jumping up and down in his excitement when we discussed it at the supper table. But I was somewhere between paralyzed with fright and in a deep state of despondency. All my friends at school had been skipping their lunches for weeks to have enough money to get in. I knew our farm family was poor, and I couldn't imagine how we would be able to pay for the entry tickets. That three-and-a-half-mile ride into town seemed like a thousand miles, and I was worried sick and had an expressionless and blank stare. In the back seat I was pessimistic that we would be able to pay the entry fee once we arrived at the gate and some or all of us would not be allowed in. To be so close but so far and not get through the gate to see the biggest show on earth (as it was billed) was an unbearable thought. I'll never, ever forget that tormented ride into town in the back seat of the car.

We pulled into the dusty parking lot (old softball field) and we piled out of the car. I lagged with a hesitant fear as we walked toward the gate.

But to my astonishment and my forever unforgettable surprise, my Uncle Carl met us at the gate, and we all walked right in. He had paid the price for our entry fee! Our financial limitations were not a problem, we were gifted with the pass! I went crazy with excitement, the unattainable price that I was dreading was a nonissue because of the gift. Thank you, Uncle Carl, for paying the admission price that we could not pay. Wowie zowie! I was inside the gate to see the greatest show on earth.

On our journey from birth to death, we can experience the same kind of torment that I had in the back seat of the car, and sadly, most people do! The thought of not having enough goodness to pass through heaven's gate may be the greatest robber of joy on our life's journey to our death and beyond. Without the assurance that heaven awaits you because Christ paid for your ticket, and you have accepted it by accepting him, your life can be filled with a shadow of an ever-present fear of dying. For the unsaved, death is a stalker which they try to fight off as long as possible because of their lack of readiness to die. We view death differently when we are ready to die and it is no longer the end, but the beginning of glory! We will make it to the circus!

If that is the case in your life, and you know what it means to dodge the subject of death, and the subject of hell is completely off limits to talk about or even think about, you are like I was in the back seat of the car. Many find it easier to just deny the existence of hell, but it is always in the back of their minds. Whether they are willing to admit it or not, knowing that... *it is appointed unto men once to die, but after this the judgment.* (Heb 9:27, KJV), we quickly become as I was in the back seat of the car, filled with panic, heading to that inevitable gate with uncertainty, as opposed to having absolute assurance enabling us to daily enjoy our matchless love gift of salvation. This enables us see death becoming an exciting transition to a place God describes as:

> *Eye hath not seen, nor ear heard, neither have entered into the heart of man, the things which God hath prepared for them that love Him.*
> (1 Cor 2:9, KJV)

I can't wait for that next eternal chapter in my life. Having this kind of hope is the gift of having joy insurance. There is not a day, and on some days, perhaps not an hour, but what this question echoes in my mind. As I get older, or when things get harder, I feel the need to escape more often. I love to dream of heaven and think how things will finally be made right. There will be no more injustice, no more unfairness, no more being misunderstood, no more experiencing the feeling of creeping diminishment, no more becoming overlooked or irrelevant, no more helplessness to do anything about it, no more rejection and no more weaknesses, knowing that in heaven as I'm looking into the beautiful, accepting eyes of my Lord, I am completely loved because I'm completely forgiven and completely seen as worthy, allowing me to be totally embraced by the Lord of lords. For a reinvigorating split second, my mind and heart escape to heaven where I can get a strong dose of instant healing and empowerment to return to earth's reality where God calls me to reengage in the sinful messiness of living on earth, where, in his behalf, I can touch hurting people with heaven's finger and bring hope where there is none.

Taking heavenly mental trips is healthy; that's why Jesus told us about it. He wants us to do it! He made it so real, so inviting, and so very personal. He knew how very required it is to have these instant mental escapes and how much this heavenly vision seared into our minds and hearts is needed to keep our hope alive. He said it this way:

> *"Do not let your hearts be troubled. You believe in God; believe also in me. My father's house has many rooms; if that were not so, would I have told you that I am going there to prepare a place for you? And if I go and prepare a place for you, I will come back and take you to be with me that you also may be where I am."* (John 14:1–3, NIV)

The poorest people on earth are those who cannot take these mental journeys to heaven, their eternal home. They live in a hopeless spiritual desert. Until they come to a personal saving and satisfying faith in Christ, they are destined to desperately grab anything that can get them through the moment. Their future is bleak, and their fear of death is even bleaker. They don't know what it means to escape and reengage. That is not an option to them. They, of all people, need to be pitied and objects of our compassion.

These dreams and these heavenly visions are lofty breaks where real spiritual change can happen in our daily lives. Just look at Peter, who misjudged his own ability and with his false self-confidence bragged how he would never turn his back on Christ, only to embarrassingly deny him three consecutive times before the crowing of the cock. But after hearing these words of Christ, and knowing what heaven held for him, Peter led in the establishment of the Church which is still growing and changing lives today.

To keep a heavenly perspective on our journey, regardless of our age, we need to be reminded what life is all about, and more importantly, where

Getting God's Big Picture Right

it is leading and where we will all end up. This ensures a joy in our journey. To that end, this book was designed and written.

Getting older is a journey from here to there, from where we are today to where we will be one thousand years from now. That may seem like a long time, but that is man's measurement of time. God's timing is very different: In a snap of the finger and a blink of an eye, we will be there.

> *But, beloved, be not ignorant of this one thing, that one day is with the Lord as a thousand years, and a thousand years as one day.* (2 Pet 3:8, KJV)

God wants us to be conscious of the speed of life, perhaps so we can endure suffering, grief, and hardships knowing it will soon be over. Or perhaps he wants us to be conscious of how little time we have to check out Jesus and accept his unrelenting efforts to love us into the next world. Either way, God wants us to know and hear the journey clock ticking. Tick, tick, tick . . .

Our journey has begun! And as with any journey, there are things we must do and prepare for to ensure a fulfilling and memorable journey that guarantees a successful journey's end. We must get there and stand before our Lord and hear him say: . . ."*Well done, good and faithful servant; thou hast been faithful over a few things, I will make thee ruler over many things: enter thou into the joy of thy lord.*" (Matt 25:23, KJV) To accomplish your successful journey, this book is intended to provide you bite-sized spiritual snacks to blunt life's hunger pains and provide critical guidance as you come to those surprising forks in the road where you have tough decisions to make. I've called these spiritual snacks journey joy makers. Don't eat them all at once, eat them one at a time, pondering and digesting them well. I've also alternated every chapter with a journey joy killer. These chapters are designed for you to be warned that something needs to be taken out of your life so joy can return or come in. After each journey joy killer and joy maker section, you are provided a way to journal your journey thoughts. If you are traveling life's journey with others, and I hope you are, use the journal area for the basis for your group discussions and prayers.

Part B: Journey Joy Maker One

I Am Heaven Bound

You can discourage me, or you can put me down,
but I know where healing and true joy can always be found.

It is not with the words of man that can often be terse, filled with hate and disgust,
but to Jesus my Lord I can and often go to find His restorative words that I trust.

God will mend my broken heart, and forgive my failures as a human being,
because His Son, Jesus died for me and took me into his forever family for total healing.

I have a grace-based guarantee that assures my eternal security,
from the fear of death and hell, I now have total immunity.

The promise of heaven makes life worth living and hardships worth enduring.
Knowing one day there will be an end to it all,
gives me hope and comfort that is so reassuring.

Yes, I am now irrevocably heaven bound,
because that is where my heavenly Father and Jesus are found.

Getting God's Big Picture Right

My Journal for My Journey

When I think about standing at heaven's gate, I am confident because of . . .

My life is full of joy because I'm traveling this road with Jesus. He makes me . . .

The promises in which I believe include . . .

I believe God wants me to think and pray about these heartfelt concepts discussed in this section.

2

God's Way of Having a Bold Self-Confidence

IN WORKING WITH CHRISTIANS, I have been surprised by the number of people who have gotten assurance of their salvation, the subject of Chapter 1, but still carry around with them a shame that prevents them from initiating bold projects and starting bold conversations for and with Christ. This chapter has been designed to show you that you may be leaving some of God's abundant, loving truths on the table.

Part A will go into the difference between guilt and shame. It is entirely possible to have been forgiven and still have a debilitating sense of shame. Many do not understand the difference between guilt and shame and their impact on their life. Most sins of omission are committed because of shame's negative influence on our decision not to initiate positive actions forward due to lack of boldness. If this is you, please give special attention to Part A in this chapter. You may even be inclined to memorize some of lines in the poem at its conclusion.

Part B provides the rationale of why we believe what we do and why we live the way that we do. Pay close attention to its contents. When you have a friend who is on your heart and you are unsure of their relationship with Christ, all you have to do is ask them this simple question: "May I ask you where you are on your spiritual journey?" I have found this question does not put a person into a defensive mode and ignites a beautiful and transparent discussion. You will find lots of information in this section that will enable you to have a great talk with a non-believer. (As an added idea, you may want to write your own why you believe note and give it to

God's Way of Having a Bold Self-Confidence

your children so that they can carry in the front of their Bibles. And when they are old enough, work with them to write their own why I believe note. These documents should be passed down from generation to generation.)

In his mighty love and grip,

LaVon

Part A

Journey Joy Killer Two

Escaping Shame

How to Become Fiercely Engaged in Living

WHETHER IT'S JUST FOR a day, a week, or a whole lifetime, nothing is worse than living in shame. Shame is a powerful emotion that can cause you to feel defective, unacceptable, even damaged beyond repair. Shame often leads one to hide and self-conceal all the giftedness God has given you. Shame has a way of putting on the brakes, bringing new and noble initiatives to a standstill because of a false sense of shamefulness (unworthiness). If you feel shame, you will hide from community and friendship. Shame will crush your spirit and inflict self-doubt. You will avoid taking risks or being vulnerable and therefore people will never see or know your true self because of your reluctance to lead. You will run from shadow to shadow, and the world will miss your very important existence, the very reason God put you in this place at this time. Shame is so powerful; it can impact the whole trajectory of your life. That is precisely why and how Satan uses this Joy Killer to destroy and demoralize us and turn us into the walking dead.

To escape it, we first must define it. We need to know what it is, and just as importantly, what it is not. We cannot attack that which we do not understand, nor pray for our protection against Satan's fiery darts if we cannot or do not recognize shame's evil when we see it. Shame could well be the greatest cause of sins of omission in your life. Shame can and will cower you into the darkness and all the good that you could and should be doing will not get done. Shame causes wasted lives and unreached people that God providentially brings across our paths as we are hampered by shame, allowing them to pass us by, unloved. I am praying that, with the help of God and his grace, we will define and defeat it and the curse it puts on our lives! Consider praying this prayer with me: Dear heavenly father, please help me defeat Satan's shame and the emotional toxicity that it spews into my life. Free me from shame, in the powerful name of Jesus, amen.

Often guilt and shame are used together in the same sentence and in the same breath. People treat them as synonymous. But they are not, they are two separate states of feeling from two different emotional conditions. Here is a chart that can assist you in identifying and recognizing which is which and how they are very different, both in cause and solution.

The Distinguishing Differences Between Guilt and Shame

Guilt	Shame
Guilt is a private experience caused by internal conflict about my personal morality.	Shame is a public experience caused by the probable or real reactions of others, if they knew.
The feeling of guilt comes from believing I've done something wrong, illegal, unbiblical, bad, or sinful.	The feeling of shame comes from the belief that I am basically flawed, inadequate, undeserving, or not good enough.
Guilt is a specific sense of transgression.	Shame is a general feeling of inadequacy.
Guilt is a focus on behavior.	Shame is a focus on self.
When I experience guilt, I've made a judgment that I've committed a wrong deed. I've done a bad thing.	When I experience shame, I've concluded that my whole self is wrong. I'm a bad person.
Guilt can be eliminated through my repentance and acceptance of forgiveness based on the work that Christ did in my behalf. This is the very work that I could not do for myself. I accept by faith God's unmerited forgiveness bestowed to me by his grace. Based on my relationship with Jesus Christ, I am not condemned. Therefore, I can and will stand guilt free!	Shame demands a reversal of my accusing self-perception by faith in God's creative design for my life and His ongoing sanctification work that was triggered by my salvation. I accept by faith my goodness in God's eyes and his high-value plan for my life. He will not waste me nor discount my relevance to this world. Therefore, I can and will stand shame free!

Part A: Journey Joy Killer Two

In addition to the individualized definitions above, here are seven salient facts about guilt and shame that will assist you in knowing where and when to look for the revolting consequences of each of these Satan-inspired and man-caused conditions.

- You can, and often do, have both guilt and shame at the same time (a double whammy).
- But it is also possible that you can have shame without guilt, and often do.
- If both are present, guilt usually precedes shame, but shame often remains after guilt is absolved through forgiveness.
- Shame has many causes other than guilt.
- Both guilt and shame are debilitating to joyful living and are core foundational contributors to many other devastating psychological disorders.
- Both guilt and shame are induced by any one of these three sources or some combination of all three:
  - The world's pressure all around you
  - Your own deceitful heart or sinful nature within you
  - Satan and his demonic network aimed at you

Note: We are three-way targeted, every day in every way. For us not to be terrified by this reality is naive. For us not to put on the full armor of God to protect ourselves is sheer foolishness on our part. (See Ephesians 6,)

- The only sure and permanent solution to guilt and shame is your personal acknowledgement of the atoning work of Jesus Christ in your behalf and the humble acceptance of his loving work applied to your heart, mind, and soul. It is believing God created you perfectly for the purpose He had in mind for you when He put you on planet earth at this exact time. (You can sing the song "Amazing Grace" right here.)

These two curses of Satan, guilt and shame, were first thrust into our lives and into our world in the garden of Eden (Genesis 3). Adam and Eve caused and experienced both of these spiritual disorders. Because of it, paradise was lost, living was permanently doomed to end badly, death came into our vocabulary, planet Earth became cursed, and all humanity was irreversibly launched in the direction of hell. Guilt and shame had turned our world order upside down. Evil had been unleashed and all hope was lost. Our futures were turned bleak and black. Satan had successfully soiled God's new and perfectly created world. The power of guilt and shame began ruling human hearts. Satan had won the battle . . . but not the war, for then came Jesus!!!!

Seeing us in the horrible bondage of guilt and shame and filled with compassion over our hopeless and ruined lives which caused the complete annihilation of his heavenly Father's personal and desired goal of spending eternity with each of us in heaven, Christ could not restrain himself. Captivated by the guilty and dejected looks in our guilt-ridden and shame-filled eyes while we were at the same time being ruthlessly marched by Satan towards the burning fires of hell, Jesus stood and left his heavenly throne, forfeiting all glory and all heavenly privileges. He came to us in a manger for the single purpose of growing up sin-free and dying and resurrecting to free each of us from Satan's dreadful and enslaving bondage of guilt and shame. Jesus was pronounced guilty by the Jewish and Roman rulers and shamed by the angry mobs screaming untruthful insults. And in that moment of time, he took all our guilt and shame from each of us and transferred them to himself. With a love so strong that he did not flinch, hesitate, or waver, like a helpless lamb, he was led to Calvary and was slaughtered.

The torturous repulsion that Father God felt caused him to turn his head and eyes away from his own son because all our despicable guilt and shame now accumulated and heaped on his own son's head. For the first time ever, Jesus was now completely alone, while at the same time feeling the combined weight of all our guilt and shame. Even then, all alone under these deplorable conditions, Jesus still resisted the temptation to call ten thousand angels to his own rescue. Instead, he willingly bowed his head and allowed the soldiers to drive the nails into his trembling hands. Enduring the pulsating pain of his torn flesh and his twitching muscles, he willingly succumbed to the horrible, humiliating, and murderous death on the cross. Being plunged into death and the grave, and with our eternities at stake, he fought the most intense and consequential three day war of all time, in which he defeated Satan and emerged on day three from the grave as the comprehensive, undeniable, and total victor over the evil curses and consequences of guilt and shame. Man's guilt-free innocence and shame-free dignity had been restored and is now lovingly available to all who accept Jesus as their Lord and Savior! And because of Jesus each of us can now defeat and completely eradicate, our own personal guilt and shame and reverse all their devastating consequences.

This was and is the turning point of all human history. One cannot point to another event that has and continues to impact more lives than this single event. Nothing compares to the breadth, depth, width, and height to which the impact of this event reaches and has more power to change people, families, and nations.

Had Jesus not done this, I could not be writing this to you now. I was guilty and I suffered from shame, and secretly felt inadequate to others, and hid in the shadows expecting and hoping someone would discover me and tell the world how good I was. I was looking for permission from man (the wrong place) to be myself, the person God created me to be. I simply did not believe in myself enough to stand tall and lead. Only God knows the number of sins of omission I've committed because I did not have the self-worth or faith to step forward and respond to the call of God and the glaring needs of those he brought across my path. My shame kept me quiet and uninvolved in the crises around me. I played it safe. Satan's shame had silenced me. But thanks be to God, Christ is setting me free! Please give me permission to tell you how. But first, read this Scripture that took place the night Jesus was being taken into custody just before His crucifixion.

The Look!

> ... Peter sat down among them. Then a servant girl, seeing him as he sat in the light and looking closely at him, said, "This man also was with him." But he denied it, saying, "Woman, I do not know him." And a little later someone else saw him and said, "You also are one of them." But Peter said, "Man, I am not." And after an interval of about an hour still another insisted, saying, "Certainly this man also was with him, for he too is a Galilean." But Peter said, "Man, I do not know what you are talking about." And immediately, while he was still speaking, the rooster crowed. And the Lord turned and looked at Peter. And Peter remembered the saying of the Lord, how he had said to him, "Before the rooster crows today, you will deny me three times." And he went out and wept bitterly. (Luke 22:55–62, ESV)

Before you go any farther, stop immediately and answer this question. When Jesus looked at Peter after he had denied him the third time, and

God's Way of Having a Bold Self-Confidence

hearing the crowing of the rooster, what did the face of Jesus look like when you pictured him in your own mind?

Was it one or more of these?

(Check the ones that mirror the images of the look of Jesus in your mind.)

- Was it a look of scolding disgust?
- Was it a look of condemnation, implying How could you have done that to me?
- Was it a look of sadness and disappointment, implying Are you really that weak of a person or love me that little?
- Was it a look of being displeased or appalled by him and what he just did, implying, you are not good enough to be my disciple?"
- Was it a look of being repulsed and upset implying, he doesn't want to have a continued relationship with him?
- Was it a look of being offended by what Peter did and letting him know how bad it made him feel?
- Was it a look of, "I told you so, you should have listened to me?"
- Was it a look of, you should really be ashamed of yourself, how can you live with yourself?

Or was it one or more of these?

- Was it a look of understanding and sympathetic love?
- Was it a look of continued confidence implying, "I still believe in you, Peter?"
- Was it a look of compassion implying, I'm sorry that happened and how are you now feeling, allow me to help you?
- Was it a look of mercy and forgiveness implying, "I hurt for you and with you?"
- Was it a look of, "Peter, I still believe in you, let's start over and go forward?"

Part A: Journey Joy Killer Two

- Was it a look of pity and sadness as to how Peter was going to feel once he thought it through?
- Was it a look of, "Yes that was bad, but I'm about to die for that kind of wrongdoing so you can be forgiven and become empowered by the Holy Spirit to become "shame free" and stronger next time?"
- Was it a look of, "I still want a forever relationship with you, do you want that also?"

What did you see in your mind's eye when you first read that passage? This is a serious and important question; don't skip over this. Think it through and check the options above that describe what you see in the face of Jesus as he looked at Peter after he denied him three times. How you portray the look of Jesus and what you envisioned in your mind reveals a great deal about your discernment and understanding of Christ. It determines the very foundation of the type and quality of your relationship with him. Your perception of Jesus governs how you respond to him daily. It reveals what kind of Jesus you believe in. It also discloses how much, if any, of a distorted view you have of who Jesus is, that Satan has been able to infest and infiltrate into your thinking.

And as you do this be reminded that in 2 Corinthians 4:4, we are told that Satan seeks to blind us so we don't see the gospel of the glory of Christ. In other words, Satan will do everything possible to keep you from seeing the loving, captivating, and inviting beauty in the face of Christ every time you think of him. He wants you to see one of those nine pictures of Jesus that appear above the line on the list of options above. This would make sure you don't think about him or talk to him in prayer, and not read his love book to you (Bible). He knows it would make you afraid of Jesus or just dislike him. He does not want you to see any of those nine options below the line. Why? Because that would make Jesus irresistible, you would run to him and invite him to be the Lord of your life. You would never want to be away from Him. You would want to fill every moment of every day with his presence! That, my friend, is the power of the beauty and wonder of who Jesus is!

> If any of you lacks wisdom, you should ask God, who gives generously to all without finding fault, and it will be given to you.

But there are many different causes of shame other than committing sins. Peter did something wrong, so his immediate weeping and repentance were in order. And that is what all of us should do when sins are committed. But what about having shame when no sins are committed? Some of you reading this book have been verbally abused and your self-esteem has been shattered or even destroyed. Others were bullied on the school ground and all these years later, they can still hear those voices echoing in their minds. They may have used some of the very words in those nine options above the line in the list we just went through. Others of us were shamed by our parents, who were probably shamed by their parents. We may have been told we were no good, or we will never amount to anything. Others of us may have had a verbally abusive manager, or even been fired. And the list goes on and on.

Then there are those voices in our heads that shame us when we look in the mirror and it is apparent: we will never be Miss or Mr. America. Or we may use some of the very same words in that list when talking to ourselves when we fail at something. Regardless of the source, the answer is always the same—Jesus. Each of is good enough, important enough, pretty/handsome enough, smart enough, and talented enough to serve in the plans he has for each of us. It is his presence in our lives connected to our presence in his life that is the answer to both guilt and shame. Read it for yourself... *With God on our side like this, how can we lose? If God didn't hesitate to put everything on the line for us, embracing our condition and exposing himself to the worst by sending his own son, is there anything else he wouldn't gladly and freely do for us?... Do you think anyone is going to be able to drive a wedge between us and Christ's love for us? There is no way! Not trouble, not hard times, not hatred, not hunger, not homelessness, not bullying threats, not backstabbing, not even the worst sins listed in Scripture ... None of this fazes us because Jesus loves us. I'm absolutely convinced that nothing—nothing living or dead, angelic or demonic, today or tomorrow, high or low, thinkable or unthinkable—absolutely nothing can get between us and God's love because of the way that Jesus our master has embraced us.* (Rom 8:31-32, 35, 37-39, MSG)

And you can take that to the bank!

Part A: Journey Joy Killer Two

Shame Free

I live in America where popularity is the name of the game,
nobody wants to be with a guy who hangs his head in shame.

The world can't tell what I'm feeling by looking on my outside,
they can only guess and conclude that I am confident in my stride.

But deep inside I have ugly, besetting feelings of inadequacy,
and if they only knew, they would stop their words of advocacy.

My noisy feelings of low self-worth and self-doubt must be hid.
So, I run from shadow to shadow lest anyone see them, God forbid.

But then I met Jesus whose unconditional love was hard for me to grasp and apprehend.
Learning of his sacrifice for me, he quickly became both my Savior and friend.

His belief in me unchained and released me from my negative feelings and set me free.
By the power of the His Holy Spirit,
I can now dream and be whatever he wants me to be.

Shame has been conquered and by his grace I can now smile and stand tall,
I will live with his confidence, until I get to heaven when there I will have it all.

But for now, I'm gushing with praise for Jesus who rescued and restored me,
and from the tyranny of shame, thank God, I have now forever been set free.

God's Way of Having a Bold Self-Confidence
My Journal for My Journey

Areas of shame in my life that I want to be free from are . . .

Shame is a Joy Killer because it causes me to . . .

I want to assist others in conquering their shame, but . . .

I plan on staying shame free by . . .

Part B

Journey Joy Maker Two

Defining a Roadmap for Your Life Journey

Why I Live the Way I Do

WE HAVE ALL HEARD the saying, "If you don't know where you are going, any road will get you there." And like lots of old sayings, there is some real wisdom in that. Like you, I've contemplated where I want to end up in life, and the clearer I became concerning that goal, the more meaningful my journey became. And oddly enough, the times it became clearest as to where I wanted to end up was when I got off course. As pieces of my own fabricated life goals came tumbling down and I became engulfed in suffering and difficulties of some kind, I became devastated and confused. Oh, don't misunderstand me. I wasn't devastated over the bad stuff happening to me (although it was gosh awful), the real root of my devastation was the realization of where the course I was on would end up taking me. That scared the hell out of me. (Pun well intended.) Where I really wanted to end up only became clearer when I began to understand where I *didn't* want to end up. Does that make sense to you? Or it became very apparent as to where I would end up if I didn't make some major mid-course corrections. As it turned out, I was living for me. I had become the center of my universe. And because I'm obviously a slow learner, I made other poor judgments more than once, all to my guilt and shame. God had mercy on me.

I suppose I wasn't so different than some or many of you, although I may have been more prideful, to my shame. I had trouble figuring out this God thing and even more trouble reaching reliable conclusions about both heaven and hell. Long story shortened, I realized that God was a huge

God's Way of Having a Bold Self-Confidence

interruption as to how I wanted to live. I had become my own "god" and I was calling the shots as to how to live life. Or at least how I felt I should live, which turned out to be how I wanted to live. It was only after I was broken and experienced failure that I realized that I had a stubborn rebellion problem, not an intellectual proof of God's existence problem. I, like a lot of people, was hiding behind a head problem when I really had a heart problem. Once I asked him in all sincerity if he was really there and if he was hearing me, and that he would please begin to reveal his reality to me. Things began to happen. Yes, I read some apologetics books, and even studied evolution. But most importantly, I said lots of simple prayers, asking for wisdom, and asking God to show himself to me. He did just that and here are the facts and realizations which I ended up believing. It would be an understatement to say that the conclusions I reached were life changing. They turned my world upside down by turning me and my thinking upside down. I share them only to satisfy your possible curiosity and show just one way it can happen to one individual. Each of us will come to the conclusions about God, heaven and hell, and who is Jesus the Christ, in our own way. So, I'm not suggesting this is a road map that everybody should follow, it is just a quick, abbreviated summary of my personal road map that resulted in turning my life upside down, which is really right side up: (concluding this roadmap was a real Joy Maker)

- I'm a nature guy, and I could not walk through the woods or look at the night sky without concluding that there had to be someone behind all this beauty and intricate design. The presence of God became revealed to me from the sheer organized exquisiteness of nature. A design denotes a designer; who but an intelligent God could pull off a drop-dead gorgeous sunset, let alone create a flower? Random chance made no sense to me. Believing in blind chance takes way more faith than I could ever possibly have. Besides that, it dehumanizes people and robs us of our dignity by cancelling out the truth that we are a unique and specially created person designed by God for his exclusive plan for our lives. I found all of this very unsettling.

- I had a hard time believing in the Bible but learning that it took forty some writers in sixty-six books, over 1500 years, and it all fits together perfectly, was mind boggling. And on top of all of that, it contained absolutely no errors, all the prophecies written and fulfilled left me with the only conclusion being that there is something uniquely different and special about this book. Archaeologists continue to uncover ancient artifacts that prove and validate the Bible's accuracy and authenticity. Skeptical historians are shocked on a regular basis over the veracity of the factual history contained in the Bible and verified in archeological digs. There is just something miraculous about this book of books. In fact, there is significantly more documentation (manuscripts) for the books of the Bible than there are for other historically recognized authors and literature, such as Plato and *The Iliad*. The more I studied it, the more I knew it was God's word, not of mere men. For my life to be optimized, I could no longer justify leaving it unread.

- And then there is this person, Jesus, who could not be overlooked. He is the central person around which the entire Bible revolves. What an astounding person. He is the recognized turning point of all history (BC, AD). There is no one as wise as is he, no one as well documented as this person called Jesus. The wisdom of his teachings is unmatchable, and his life was impeccable. There are hundreds of times more evidence for him and what he did than people like Socrates or Aristotle. Then to top it all off, he arose from the grave. He could not and must not be ignored by me any longer. He became a major, indisputable, historical fact that called for my close attention and concentration. I could not be considered an honest person if I didn't get to know and come- o terms with this guy called Jesus, the Christ, the Son of the living God who had the bold audacity to say things like, *"I am the way, and the truth, and the life. No one comes to the Father except through me"*. (John 14:6, ESV)

- I had to decide. Was he a phony liar, or could he be telling the truth? I couldn't run from that question any longer, I had to make a decision. The risks for not knowing him were way too high.

- Once I became intellectually forced to recognize Jesus for who he was and is, and I studied him more, the more I fell emotionally in love with his love for me. I had never experienced or seen a love like that before. he blew me away, and he still does! He simply became irresistible and I ended up giving my life and future to him. Even more remarkable, he accepted me, little old me. Unequivocally, he is now my Lord, Savior, and best friend. Period! This will go down as the single best decision of my entire life! My only regret is why in the world did it take me so long to reach these conclusions?

God's Way of Having a Bold Self-Confidence

- And one final thing. God, the Bible, Jesus, and the Holy Spirit, when all combined, form the answers to the greatest mysteries of life. They paint the big picture of the world and life in it. Nothing else, no philosophy or religion, enables life to make any sense other than the Bible. It speaks to the condition of the human soul in a way that has life-changing impact on individuals from all cultures, nations, and walks of life. The Bible text allows everything about life's meaning and purpose to be explained. I can't get over how deep and how complete this book is. I've now been studying it for years and I feel like I've just scratched its surface. The Bible's view and wisdom for living is unmatchable. It is enabling me to make sense out of how to live life to the max. Without it, not only would I be a complete wreck, but I would still be like a little lost puppy bouncing and crashing off walls. I needed and wanted the answers to life's most serious questions like:

  - Who am I?
  - From where did I come?
  - Why am I here?
  - What should living my life be all about?
  - Where am I going?

Until we have answers to these questions, our souls will remain constantly restless, and in the absence of these answers, all hope vaporizes at the very times we need it most. These questions demand that we answer them, or they will haunt us in the stillness of the middle of the night. Without believable, credible, and meaningful answers, life becomes empty, hollow, and often not even worth living at all. All other options for living become nothing more than cheap distractions. I wanted the real thing and would not settle for anything less. I wanted answers, real answers, defensible answers, that could and would weather the strongest storms of life. I wanted my life to be built on solid truth, and I ended up finding it to be God's truth, in the Bible!

The five simple and summarized facts above tell my story of how and why I'm a sold-out believer in Jesus Christ and the Bible. They have now formed the foundation of my life. Once I came to these conclusions, I then began turning my attention to all the things that the Bible teaches about life which became and still is becoming *Joy Makers for Your Life Journey*. This book is dedicated to sharing some of the most impacting ah-ha moments

Part B: Journey Joy Maker Two

that I've discovered. I refer to them as journey joy makers. Life with Christ was intended to be a thrilling and joyful adventure. As you read this book, buckle up; you are in for a ride. If you are anything like me, you are about to go down some paths that you did not even know existed. Enjoy and be amazed by his plan for your life.

> *For I know the plans I have for you, declares the LORD, plans for welfare and not for evil, to give you a future and a hope.* (Jeremiah 29:11, ESV)

God's Way of Having a Bold Self-Confidence

The Story of Me

He designed me for me and gave me to me,
He implanted my potential into me even though it I could not see.
He set me on a course that was designated only for me,

So I wouldn't lose my way, he gave me the Holy Spirit whose guidance would be key,
to fulfill my potential is the way it was intended to be.
But I got lost because my focus was entirely on me.
To my guilt and shame, I had made a mess of me,
but by the power of his love, I repented, and he heard my plea.

And now through grace and for the second time he regave me to me,
first born of the flesh, now born of the Spirit honoring my request on bended knee.

Thank you, Jesus, for giving me back to me
And in my new wisdom, I'm giving me to thee.

And may it always be,
for all eternity!

Part B: Journey Joy Maker Two

My Journal for My Journey

The real reason I am who I am and do what I do is . . .

The way I came to these conclusions is . . .

What and who motivates me most is . . .

I will write my own version of this Joy Making chapter and give it to my children that can be passed down through the generations, I will have it done by_____

3

Defying Sin's Gravitational Pull Downward

THAT GIANT GRAVITATIONAL PULL you feel constantly dragging you downward is coming straight from hell. We've all known from childhood that heaven is up, and hell is down. The Bible uses the same directional imagery of up being associated with God and good. Jesus, said: *"And I, when I am lifted up from the earth, will draw all people to myself."* (John 12:32, ESV)

The Bible uses phrases like down to Sheol, or down to the pit, to symbolize the place of the wicked and evil. This chapter makes use of these same directional metaphors. These directions have emotional reality like, down in the mouth, feeling down, our heads hang down. Likewise for up: things are looking up, Are you feeling up today? Are you up for it?

Part A will delve into the causes of the three steps down. The steps were devised and first used by Satan and he still uses the three same steps on each of us today. It is frightening how many of us succumb to his methodology without even knowing it was designed by Satan. I think once you see it and understand it, you will be able to see what Satan is doing and resist it. It is imperative that he gets us to take that first step in order to get us to sin. These three steps may be the most important concepts in this book. Please try very hard to understand their significance of how Satan will get most of the people in the world to go to hell, and this is not an overstatement.

Part B will take you in the exact opposite direction. It will lift you up into heavenly realms where you can enjoy an intimacy with God that you may have never known before. We were made for closeness to God through Christ, and yet it doesn't always feel as though we can grasp God's nearness to us. Though God desires intimacy and fellowship with us, it's not

Part B: Journey Joy Maker Two

uncommon for us to feel as though he is distant. I pray that this section will assist you in breaking through any barriers prohibiting closeness with the one who loves you more than anyone.

Enjoy these two very opposite sections!

In his mighty love and rip,

LaVon

Part A

Journey Joy Killer Three

The Three Slippery Steps Descending Down

Where May I Have Gone Wrong?

THE STREET TALK CONSENSUS is that the millennials are the entitled generation. I think it is unwise and unfair to brand a whole generation as entitled. People are individuals, some may or may not feel entitled. But I am happy that in the last number of years, the word *entitlement* has been brought into vogue in our public discourse. We've needed to focus on that intrinsic motivation that so many of us have, and to which any of us can very easily fall prey, not just millennials. I think that some of us baby boomers have a bigger problem with it than do the millennials, but that's a discussion for another day. Entitlement is certainly not a new concept. Adam and Eve were told by Satan that they were entitled to have the forbidden fruit of the tree of life, and now the rest is history, a bad history in which we all must pay a price for the evil that was unleashed way back in the Garden of Eden. The reason they ate of the forbidden fruit was because as they were reaching up to pick it, they were thinking, "Forget the prohibition commanded by God, we are entitled to have this fruit. We won't allow God to make us victims and not get what we deserve." Read it for yourself and see if you can figure out how Satan made them feel like victims, then moved them to feeling entitled, and underscored both the victim and the entitlement feelings that he was able to instill in them. If you can ascertain how he set up and knocked down Eve, you will also see how he can, and perhaps is, doing it to you.

Part A: Journey Joy Killer Three

> *Now the serpent was more crafty than any other beast of the field that the Lord God had made. He said to the woman, "Did God actually say, 'You shall not eat of any tree in the garden'?" And the woman said to the serpent, "We may eat of the fruit of the trees in the garden, but God said, 'You shall not eat of the fruit of the tree that is in the midst of the garden, neither shall you touch it, lest you die.'" But the serpent said to the woman, "You will not surely die. For God knows that when you eat of it your eyes will be opened, and you will be like God, knowing good and evil." So when the woman saw that the tree was good for food, and that it was a delight to the eyes, and that the tree was to be desired to make one wise, she took of its fruit and ate, and she also gave some to her husband who was with her, and he ate.* (Genesis 3:1–6, ESV)

I submit for your consideration that this type of thinking you just read from the book of Genesis is exactly what goes through our own minds just before we commit sins, any sin, big or small. We play the victim entitlement card and psychologically, by becoming a victim first, it seemingly gives us permission to feel entitled and to proceed to do something we know is wrong. The two strongest Satan-whispered phrases for inspiring a person to sin, are, "You're a victim and therefore, you're entitled." It's a two-step process that leads to sinning and eventually to hell itself. If you stop step #1 (I am a victim.) you will thereby prevent step 2 (Therefore I'm entitled to . . .) To annihilate victim thinking must be every child of God's goal. To destroy our lives, Satan must first get us to think we are victims. Once he succeeds in that, he's got us. He now has us on the slippery slope descending into hell. In case you are wondering, and to be perfectly clear, you can be victimized, but you don't ever have to feel like a victim. Victims are people who have no God. If you have an active relationship with God, who is your personal heavenly Father, you never ever need to feel like a victim. Yes, I said *never*! (To understand this vital concept and to learn how to build an immunity against victim thinking, read joy maker seven in this book.)

And then there is step three. The world gave it a name—narcissism. This is another word that increased in its popularity in the last several years. It is more and more common for people to label other people a narcissist. Narcissism, which I am calling step three, is nothing more than entitlement on steroids. It is when entitlement is now out of control and has begun controlling your life. The narcissist may feel entitled to act out in any numbers of ways, ways that he or she would never tolerate from anyone else. The

Defying Sin's Gravitational Pull Downward

truth is narcissism is about taking, and it's also about acting out behavior without an understanding of regarding its impact on others.

Do you get and see the descending and Joy Killing sequence?

- Step one down: Allowing yourself to slip into thinking and feeling like a victim
- Step two down: Allowing yourself to further slip into self-centered entitlement thinking
- Step three down: Allowing yourself to slip even further down and now becoming an obnoxious narcissist

Would you please consider saying this prayer with me? "Dear Father, in the next few minutes please give me the humility of doing an honest evaluation as to if or how far I may have descended down these three slippery steps so that I can call on you to purge these thoughts and feelings out of my life and restore in me a grateful spirit. In Jesus' name, amen"

The escalating consequences of moving downward by devolving towards step three becomes more and more harmful both to yourself and to everyone in your sphere of influence. Here is a partial listing of the symptoms and implications that result from this downward spiral. If someone has a narcissistic sense of entitlement, that means the person believes he or she deserves certain privileges and concessions—and they can become arrogant about it. The term "culture of narcissistic entitlement" suggests that a person will now have highly unreasonable expectations about what they are entitled to and what they feel like they deserve. As you go through this list, check every box where you feel the Holy Spirit is convicting you and you see that trait or thought pattern is beginning to take up residence in your own life. (Go slowly and prayerfully, this has serious consequences in your life.)

- You have an exaggerated sense of self-importance (pride).
- You have a sense of entitlement and require constant, excessive admiration.
- You expect to be recognized as superior even when you don't have the achievements that warrant it.
- You exaggerate your achievements and talents.
- You are preoccupied with fantasies about success, power, brilliance, beauty, or the perfect mate.

Part A: Journey Joy Killer Three

- You believe you are superior and can only associate with equally special people.
- You monopolize conversations and belittle or look down on people you may perceive as inferior.
- You expect special favors and unquestioning compliance with your expectations and have resentment when people don't meet those expectations.
- You take advantage of others to get what you want and justify it by thinking you are or have been a victim and therefor are entitled.
- You have an inability or unwillingness to recognize and/or acknowledge the needs and feelings of others.
- You are envious of others and may even delude yourself into believing others envy you.
- You behave in an arrogant or haughty manner, coming across as conceited, boastful, pretentious, and always right.
- You insist on having the best of everything—for instance, the best car, best home, best office, etc.

By attentively working through this list, you may discover that the roots of narcissism may have already found a way into some of your thinking and feelings.

At the same time, if you have or are beginning to have a narcissistic personality disorder, you will be having trouble handling anything you perceive as criticism or resistance. Check the boxes where you see signs of these occurrences in your own life.

- You become impatient or angry when you don't receive special treatment that you deserve.
- You have significant interpersonal problems and easily feel slighted.
- You react with rage or contempt and try to belittle the other person to make yourself appear superior.
- You have difficulty regulating emotions and behavior.
- You experience major problems dealing with stress and adapting to change.

Defying Sin's Gravitational Pull Downward

- You feel depressed and moody because you fall short of perfection or living up to your own expectations.
- You have secret feelings of insecurity, shame, vulnerability, and humiliation.
- You have drug or alcohol misuse.
- You have a history of relationship difficulties.
- You have ongoing people conflicts at work or school.
- You have suicidal thoughts or behavior.

In addition to the presence of the thought and behavior patterns mentioned above, there is a conspicuous absence of these life aspects in the daily life of a narcissist (sins of omission).

- The absence of sacrificial and generous giving to real needs
- The absence of compassion to those experiencing hurt, often thinking that they deserve it, or it's their self-made problem, thinking they made their bed and now they must sleep in it
- The inability or numbness to the feelings of others in your life, or a harsh lifestyle of just not giving a damn about the desires, hurts, and needs of others around you
- Oblivious to the needs of comforting, encouraging, strengthening, supporting, and inspiring those that God continuously and providently keeps bringing into our world for you to love on his behalf.

As you went through the lists above, if you got some check marks in some of the boxes, you've got some praying to do. But to get out of any uncompassionate, loveless, or cold-hearted ruts beginning to take hold that may be showing up in your life, it will take more than a few general prayers. This is a serious matter and you must give it the serious attention it deserves before it takes over more and more of your life like a cancer on your soul. If God has your attention, let's hit it head-on by getting committed to eradicating this joy killer out of your life while we can, once and for all.

To begin, you are encouraged to obtain and read my initial book specifically designed to tackle this problem. It is entitled, *Untangling the Seven Desires of Your Heart*. It is a calculated, step-by-step journey to emotional freedom. In it, you will discover that you may have any one or more debilitating love gaps that need to be closed before you can experience the freedom of becoming a more loving and lovable human being that God wants to use in a mighty way. A love gap is a self-permitted condition in anyone of seven different areas where you have yet to allow God to bless and fill you with his unconditional and liberating love. Doing so will fill you with a joy and peace that passes all understanding. (That is God's promise, not mine.) These are foundational needs that we all have and the only solution to these cries of our heart is to understand God's unique provisions for each of these seven desires that God has instilled in our lives for his divine purposes of drawing us closer and closer to him. When we learn how to invite and allow God to fill each of these love gaps, we become enabled to have a forever connection and exhilarating relationship with him.

The Bible summarizes and treats these three problems (victim thinking, self-entitlement. and loveless narcissism) as three dimensions coming out of a core problem of self-centeredness. It also characterizes the seriousness of the problem of selfishness as being ultimately self-destructive and eternally deadly.

> *"And how does a man benefit if he gains the whole world and loses his soul in the process? For is anything worth more than his soul?"* (Mark 8:36–37, TLB)

The Bible also treats selfishness as the reason that most of our problems are not being solved.

> *And even when you do ask you don't get it because your whole aim is wrong—you want only what will give you pleasure.* (James 4:3, TLB)

And finally, the Bible discloses that the ultimate remedy for selfishness is to become 100 percent surrendered and sold-out to Jesus who paved the way by first giving 100 percent of himself to each of us.

> *I have been crucified with Christ and I no longer live but Christ lives in me. The life I live in the body, I live by faith in the Son of God, who loved me and gave himself for me.* (Galatians 2:20, NIV)

Defying Sin's Gravitational Pull Downward

The Road of Love

We live in a world filled with hate and endless wars,
so many wrong paths and roads, so many wrong doors.
They all seem to lead to disappointment, disillusionment, and more worldly pain, no
fairness, no relief, no justice, and no love and hope to gain.
But then from heaven's realms there came a volunteer,
a person misunderstood and one the world would jeer.

A gentle, different kind of person from the way he was born and on to manhood,
stepping into a world of broken relationships that he came to reconcile and make good.

Not with brilliant reasoning nor with an iron clenched fist,
he would right all the wrongs with a simple love kiss.
He showed us a very different and better way to confront the world's wrongs,
not with marching armies or stern lectures, but with heartfelt love songs.

We've been visited by Jesus, the Godman, from his heavenly father's throne.
He showed us a new way to heal the conflicts of man,
a power mankind had never known.

He walked us on a new road that led us in a new and different direction,
knowing we were not strong enough to follow, he gave us his perfection.
He filled us with his Holy Spirit to guide us, preventing us from becoming lost
down a road we would have never imagined; it was the way of the cross.
And now on wings of angels we travel through the thorny issues of life,
living above the fray while being immune to all the confusion and strife.
We are walking on the road toward heaven hand in hand with Jesus our Lord,
immersed in his love and moving forward in one accord.

Part A: Journey Joy Killer Three

My Journal for My Journey

I am most vulnerable to feeling like a victim when . . .

These are the entitlement feelings I'm most tempted to feel . . .

This is what I need to do to release God's compassion through me . . .

Part B
Journey Joy Maker Three

Getting Near to God

So Just How Close Are You to God Right Now?

I REMEMBER LIKE YESTERDAY, as a little boy, looking up at my aging father in the third row of our small country church, watching and listening to him sing. My elderly farmer dad, a very humble, tall, thin man with rough, callused hands holding that old, tattered hymnbook while looking to the front of the church and modestly singing in his deep voice: *Nearer, my God, to Thee, nearer to Thee* . . . (and then bellowing out) *Still all my song shall be, nearer, my God, to Thee.* I saw the emotion in his eyes. I felt the confidence and safeness in his heart that he felt in the brutal, tireless work of farming, fighting the cursed land to eke out and sustain the existence of his large family of seven children. I remember him losing the corn crop one year to the armyworm and the wheat crop to a windstorm. But still, through it all, he remained rock-solid and confident in God's provision. He was and is my hero, and it was obvious that God was his hero. His favorite hymn was, "Great is thy faithfulness".

Even at my young age, it was clear to me that there was a connection between my gentle, hard-working father, who was steady as a rock, and his nearness to God. But sadly, it wasn't until many years later that I really grasped the power of that nearness to God connection. But now I know, and I can't stop talking about it.

There is a reason why the psalmist said,

> *But for me it is good to be near God; I have made the Lord God my refuge* . . . (Psalm 73:28, ESV)

Part B: Journey Joy Maker Three

Allow me to be plain-spoken about this. It's just flat out impossible to remain unshaken and peaceful in the hardest of times if you are not near to God. Which begs the question, how do you know if you are near enough to God to be mentally and emotionally resilient to all that life can and will throw at you? We are often implored to just have faith and believe things will work out okay, but we are seldom encouraged to check out our distance to or from God. Biblically speaking, it's our proximity to God that makes the difference. If the truth be told, many of us are just one step away from the most sublime peace that mankind can ever know. Even if you do believe and have faith, but you are not near to God, you are vulnerable and very defenseless.

Read and really hear this biblical Joy Making command:

Let us draw near to God with a sincere heart and with the full assurance that faith brings. (Hebrews 10:22a, NIV)

In plain English, we are being directed to get close to God. Or as the psalmist says

Under his wings you will find refuge. (Psalm 91:4b, (ESV)

Do you see that? You can believe all you want, but if you are not under his wings, you will not and cannot experience his full healing protection. None of that personal, loving protection can happen if there is distance between you and God, The Bible is clear, we are implored to (in my words) get close to God or run to Jesus. If you want to live to the max while experiencing God's loving and personal protection, we must get close to God, get under His wings. This is God's safe space, a place where anxiety is absent. This is where you are and I will feel hugged and held by God. This is counterintuitive, but you can be so close to his safety but so very far away at the very same time. Under his wings is your personal no fear zone!

I so hope you are not reading this too fast and you are pondering these critical and life-changing concepts. This is so very important to the quality of your daily life. I've witnessed a prevalent and naive attitude in many Christians. They say the right things and even pray the right things, but they are not near to God. Safety only resides under his wings or, being near to God. To God, closeness matters! If you ever wondered why so many people are susceptible to panic attacks, sleepless nights, anxious thoughts (and the list goes on and on), they are out from under his wings.

This purposely is not a hard command to obey. In fact, it is more of an invitation than it is a commandment. By his merciful design, to be under his wings is easily accomplished because his grace is the catalyst to move

Defying Sin's Gravitational Pull Downward

you in his direction. He designed it to be easy. He loves you forward. He does not want you to earn anything or prove anything. Jesus has done all of that for you. This is how being a Christian is so remarkably different than all the godless religions of the world as compared to what they require. You do not have to take a strenuous journey or some perilous pilgrimage to close the distance to end up near to God on some sacred mountain. You are just one step away! Read that again: you are just one step away. In an unbelievable and profound passage, the Bible says it so very simply, read it now. *Come near to God and he will come near to you.* (James 4:8a, NIV)

Wow! Said another way, just take one step in God's direction and he will run to you, and he will take away all the distance between you and him. Remember in Luke 15, how the father ran to the prodigal son when his father first saw him coming home? God wants to see in you the desire to be with him and trust him with your life. He wants you to show him that there is nothing to which you are clinging that would put distance between you and him. This is the invitation from you that he is eagerly waiting to see and receive before he runs to you. He wants to see that you see him as being more important than anything and anyone in this world. Let that sink in. Does your heart long to be with him? Is that what he is seeing right now as he looks in your direction? If not, how will you take that one step towards him? Maybe, like the prodigal son, you need to confess the sin(s) that separate you. Maybe you have repented of the wrong direction you've been going in life and you are now turning around and taking that one step in his direction. Or, if you don't know what's causing distance, you can ask God the Holy Spirit to show you what is separating you from him or what is keeping you from taking that one step towards him. He desires to tell and show you what is causing the distance between you and him. Distance matters to God. He wants to be near and with you far more than you will ever want to be with him. We simply are not capable of loving him as much as he loves us or desiring him as much as he desires us or treasuring him as much as he treasures us. But he is not requiring that you measure up to his standards of excellence, Jesus has already done that for you. He just wants you to look at him and take that one step in his direction. He needs to see movement towards him. He wants to see you coming home to get under his wings. Remember, he is always looking in your direction, always watching and waiting for you to take that first step in his direction. But we must go first and take that initial step towards him. God will never intrude into your

Part B: Journey Joy Maker Three

space until you first take that one step toward him. No mountains to climb, no oceans to swim, just start moving in his direction.

This is not just a one-time event. Just because you may have accepted Christ as your personal Savior some time in your past does not mean that the distance gap in your life has been forever managed for the rest of your life. I'm talking about real-time living. Or should I say real-time-sinning? And any sin, every sin, causes distance. Please take a few minutes and read 1 John, which was written precisely for the distance consequence of our daily sinning. And distance means you are out from under his wing.

This is where several biblical truths converge to form a powerful daily living process. Let's begin by putting these three certainties together in your mind:

- *Pray without ceasing,* 1 Thessalonians 5:17 (ESV)
- *If any of you lacks wisdom, let him ask God, who gives generously to all without reproach, and it will be given him* James 1:5 (ESV)
- *Draw near to God, and he will draw near to you.* James 4:8 (ESV)

Together, these three spiritual truths are the key to getting and staying close to God. They get and keep you under his wing. You can call them the "distance busters." Whenever you feel alone, anxious, helpless, guilty, shamed, weakened, threatened, angered, exposed, confused, wronged, unloved, diminished, victimized, prideful, vengeful, unforgiving, impatient, dumb, a failure, unimportant, persecuted, indecisive, etc. If you are anything like me, this abbreviated list of feelings rings lots of bells where I need some one-on-one time with God, under his wing. It should be obvious to everyone that we need a close partnership with God just to get through this earthly life.

I can attest that the combination of these biblical truths became a game-changer in my life. They solidified a beautiful, ongoing father-son relationship; it would be impossible for me to overstate how wonderful it is. I confess, I didn't pray that much even though I knew I should. I didn't have a thirst for daily Bible reading and felt guilty about it. And I didn't even know what an intimate, dynamic relationship with God felt like. I remember reading Paul's definition of what it means to be near to God and wondering what he meant by it:

For in him we live, and move, and have our being. Acts 17:28 (NIV)

Defying Sin's Gravitational Pull Downward

But now, from the time I wake up to the time I fall to sleep, I'm talking to God, we are sharing life, I love getting into his Word, I'm taking everything to him in hundreds of prayers every day. We can't stop talking. I tell him everything, all my stupid sins and thoughts. And I don't do any of this because I'm supposed to, I do it naturally every time I find myself in one of those conditions that I listed in the paragraphs above. I simply cannot live without him. Plus, I'm head-over-heels in love with him and cannot get enough of him. Those three verses keep me under his wing, my favorite place to be until I get to heaven.

I want every thought, every action, and every feeling to be in him. I want to be lost in him. When people see or hear me, I want them to see and hear Jesus. That is what Paul implies about what it is like to be near him in that text above. We give up our identity (our brand) to him. Our lifestyle is saturated by his will in our lives. We never want to be without him. Now I know what my dad felt when he sang. I wish he were still alive so I could sing it with him now. But I'm willing to wait until heaven, and the truth be told, I'll be a much better singer then. If you know the song, sing the chorus with me now.

> Nearer, my God to thee.
> Nearer to thee!
> Still all my song shall be
> Nearer, my God, to thee . . .

Part B: Journey Joy Maker Three

Nearness

Nearness to God is my destination,
for peace and protection, that's the only location.

To separate me from my Lord is Satan's trap,
but Jesus came from heaven to close the distance gap.
Now I have the privilege of being protected under his wing.
It's the place where my anxieties for removal I can bring.

It's where I experience my relationship with God's nearness,
a place where I can think and process life with his clearness.

It's a place where healing and restoration exist under his wings,
where his strength replaces my weakness that his grace brings.

When I sin and am ashamed of all my filthiness,
I go under his wings, where I emerge with his pureness.

Thank you, God, for inviting me under your wing,
for this provision, I will forever your praises sing.

Defying Sin's Gravitational Pull Downward

My Journal for My Journey

When I think about nearness to God, I feel . . .

Under his wings is where I . . .

To get and stay near to God, I . . .

These are the things the interfere with my nearness to God . . .

4

Rethinking Your Response to Sin

From our childhood, sin has always been a heavy, negative, and angry word. Just the thought of it conjures up feelings of hopelessness, disgrace, and failure. So, this chapter will have some surprises for you.

Part A will immediately take you into the world that is inside you. We've been taught that when we sin, God becomes our enemy and we feel his disgust. Oh, how wrong we've been and how we've been deceived into having the exact opposite view of God when we sin. The real truth will thrill you. I think once you see it, you will really be set free.

Part B will confront you with the motivation with which you get up and go every day. If you have ever felt that internal resistance about getting up and going into work, this section is for you. It is a short section but do not underestimate the power of being properly motivated.

In his mighty love and grip,

LaVon

Part A

Journey Joy Killer Four

Do You Have a Sinful View of Sin?

The Sinful Power of a Candy Wrapper

OUR CORPORATE OFFICE IS in twin towers joined by a large common atrium. When I leave the office for the day, I come down the elevators and walk through the large atrium past a security desk on which a big bowl of hard candies sits every evening. On this particular night they had caramel candies, my favorite. As I walked by, I reached in and grabbed one. And as I, along with a bunch of other scurrying employees, were walking through the enclosed walkway in route to the garage, I decided to unwrap the candy and put it into my mouth. In my hurried pace as part of a mob of other workers hurrying to our cars to get out of the garage first, I accidently dropped the candy wrapper on the floor of the walkway. I thought, no big deal and I kept on moving with the hustling crowd.

About twenty steps further, it hit me. What kind of person would drop litter and not pick it up? So, I did an about face and swam upstream dodging people until I found the candy's paper wrapper and picked it up and retuned back towards my car. On my 45-minute drive home, God and I had quite a talk about what I had just done. It was one of those times where I began to get new understanding as to the true nature of sin. It proved to be a real eye opener. I was unprepared to be guided by the Holy Spirit to a conclusion in which I discovered that I had an unbiblical and flawed view of sin. This may be somewhat difficult but allow me to try to explain.

You see, I thought that when I sinned, I was sinning against an angry God, and he was somehow mad, hurt, and upset with me. And worse yet, he would punish me accordingly to the size or badness of the sin. So, to lighten my conscience, I would think things like, "That sin wasn't all that bad, so God won't be all that mad." I did not know that I had a dangerous and corrupted concept of sin. I was surprised as to how far off I was, but I shouldn't have been. I knew that Satan is the father of lies, and the Bible warns us about the deceitfulness of our own hearts, and I live in a polluted world which is filled with contaminated thinking. That all adds up to becoming a three-way barrage of erroneous misinformation aimed at my concept of sin, or my understanding as to what is right versus wrong. Nor had I ever considered how my understanding of sin plays a huge and damaging role in my life. I had never thought that much about it. I just thought that sin was sin and that's all there was to it, so wrong and misdirected was I. But it doesn't take much thinking to arrive at the conclusion that Satan wants and needs us to have a distorted view of sin. Sin is evil, isn't it? Yes, a thousand times yes, but not for the reasons you may think. It's not just what sin does to God, (and even that is not what you think it is; more on that later.) it's what it does to you and me. And we must also consider what sin does for Satan. he's by far, the biggest winner when we sin. And that alone ought to bum us out.

When I dropped that candy wrapper and didn't stop to pick it up, my self-identity (both my self-image and my self-esteem) took a big hit downward. I became less than I was before I dropped the paper and decided not to pick it up. Just that little and seemingly excusable act of dropping a small candy wrapper revealed something bad about me and my thinking that I didn't want to believe about myself. It wasn't the size of the paper, or the insignificance of one little piece of paper on an already somewhat soiled walkway that made it a Joy Killer. It showed my rebellion against having to do what is right. It showed that I didn't give a darn about other people having to see and live with my litter. It showed a degree of pride whereby I could do what I want and not have to be in obedience to any laws of decency. It revealed a prideful, rebellious, and unloving heart. Yeah, I can talk to myself and attempt to belittle the misdeed, thinking I'll make up for it somehow later, but what I did was just plumb wrong, and no mental chicanery or excuses would change that, nor would they fool and silence my conscience. And I knew it, and since I must live with myself every day, I didn't want to live with a person like that. That is a real journey joy killer!

On one rainy spring afternoon, I was working with my dad on a fence line on our family farm. I had just removed some old nails in a fence post so I could apply new fencing, and without stopping work, Dad said something to this effect: "Son, you know those nails and nail holes are just like sin, and just like you now have removed those rusty old nails, God can forgive and remove your sins, but the nail holes will remain. As you get older, you don't want any nail hole scars degrading your ability to live life to the fullest." And without missing a beat, or further discussion, we went right on working. When I dropped that candy wrapper and didn't pick it up, I remembered what Dad had said, and I instantly thought of this verse:

> *You may be sure that your sin will find you out.* (Numbers 32:23b, NIV)

Sins don't disappear or just go away; each and every sin will always have consequences! By God's grace, my sins will be forgiven, and I will go on to heaven, but I don't want to have nail-hole scars that Satan can and will use to shame and negatively influence me along the way. Once you come to know that every sin will chip away at your ability and confidence to have a bold and joyous life, then sin will begin mattering to you. Sin belittles us and makes us less of a man or woman. And once you see that every sin, regardless of size, tarnishes the glory we want to give back to the Christ in whom we're head over heels in love, sin will really matter to us! Once you see that sin is exactly what Satan is looking to sneak into your life to raise hell, (pun intended), sin will really begin mattering to you. And once you see you will not be able to have either the inclination or ability to boldly love God, yourself, and others as well and as much as you did before the sin. The evilness of sin will begin to take on the importance for which God intended it to have.

Our view and ongoing fight against the pulling power of sin deserves some detailed attention. Please do a slow read of this interesting, but revealing passage on sin:

> *Dear children, do not let anyone lead you astray. The one who does what is right is righteous, just as he is righteous. The one who does what is sinful is of the devil, because the devil has been sinning from the beginning. The reason the Son of God appeared was to destroy the devil's work. No one who is born of God will continue to sin, because God's seed remains in them; they cannot go on sinning, because they have been born of God. This is how we know who the children of God are and who the children of the devil are: Anyone who does not do what is right is not God's child, nor is anyone who does not love their brother and sister.* (1 John 3:7–10, NIV)

Part A: Journey Joy Killer Four

First John has a special place in my heart. A number of years ago, it was the primary place in the Bible that I found assurance of my salvation. (Read the chapter on Journey Joy Maker One). But as you just read in these poignant verses, this same Bible book could also be used to give you assurance that you are lost and have not yet been saved because you do not have the convicting power of the Holy Spirit within you blowing the whistle on sin. If you can go on sinning and not collide with the nudging and prodding work which is the protective work of the Holy Spirit, whose job is to guard those of us who believe in Christ, then something is terribly wrong. This verse explains why I had to go back and find and pick up that candy wrapper. Think about this, it's a precious privilege to feel and experience God's intervention. Ask yourself "Why did he do it?" Not because that candy wrapper would somehow hurt him, or others, not because he was mad at me, and not because he wanted to punish me. He did it for one reason only, he loves me and wanted to protect me from myself and my relationship with him. He wants to shield me from Satan. He is against anything and everything that could damage my relationship with him. Just to experience his active, restraining guidance in my life, endears him to me more and more. What a privilege to have the God of the universe so involved in my life to protect me from something so small as dropping and not picking up a candy wrapper that would have injured my view and acceptance of myself and left me open to Satan's destructive power. God's attentiveness to me and protective involvement in my life just blows my mind. I've never had anybody who cares as much as he does about his relationship with me and is so committed to not let anything harm it or come between him and me.

Once you change your view of sin and start thinking how it impacts your all-important, life-giving relationship with Jesus, and you begin to wisely understand what sin is doing to you and how it hurts and limits your vibrant fellowship with Jesus who has died in order to have a deeply personal and intimate relationship with you, your whole approach to sin will dramatically change. You will find yourself searching for any sin that could interrupt the sweetness of your minute-by-minute relationship with Jesus. My motivation for reading the Bible took an unexpected change. I began reading the Bible to discover anything that would prevent me from experiencing Christ. I want to fill every moment of every day with his presence.

Before I discovered this truth about sin, I would think of sin as seeing Jesus glaring at me and wagging his finger at me in disgust. Hopefully, you are beginning to see that is simply not true. That is Satan's lie perpetrated on us. When I sin, Jesus is filled with sorrow that I'm moving away from our close relationship, for which he died in order to have with me. When I sin, he grieves, he looks at me longingly, his eyes cry out for me, and his broken heart yearns for me. His expression says, "LaVon, don't leave me, I love you, please stay with me!"

Is all of this making sense to you? Let's take it yet another step further; read these verses and let's ponder the wonder of God's big picture. It just keeps getting better!

> *This is how we know that we belong to the truth and how we set our hearts at rest in his presence: If our hearts condemn us, we know that God is greater than our hearts, and he knows everything. Dear friends, if our hearts do not condemn us, we have confidence before God and receive from him anything we ask, because we keep his commands and do what pleases him.* (1 John 3:19–22, NIV)

Okay, let's begin putting all of this together. Perhaps one of the top lies of Satan is to have us associate sin with condemnation connected in our minds. Satan wants us to immediately feel condemned. Once he gets us in that frame of mind, we will begin running and hiding from God, just like Adam and Eve did in the Garden of Eden because they were feeling condemned. God still came to them in the coolness of the evening and calling for them. The change was not in God, but in them. Read those verses above again. See and feel the consequences of thinking you are condemned, your loss of confidence, and unanswered prayers. (That means your communication has been interrupted.) God does not want us to live in condemnation because of the toll it takes on our relationship with him, and in addition, our relationship with ourselves. Which begs the question, How are you getting along with yourself lately? How do you feel about yourself? When we are in that awful state of feeling condemned, we can't look Jesus in the eye, we just want to hide. Look at that first line in that Scripture we just read, *set our hearts at rest in his presence*. If people only knew this, drug abuse and alcoholism would subside, and suicides would decrease. Real relief only comes when our hearts are at rest his presence. (Do you need to read this paragraph again? It contains a game-changing huge promise!)

The literal meaning of the word *sin* in the original Greek text means missing the goal. What goal is God implying when the word sin is used in the Bible? It does not mean you have just sinned, and therefore you are now on your way to hell. It does not mean that God is now extremely angry with you. No, a thousand times no. The goal that is being missed is what he had in mind when he created Adam and Eve, and the goal God had in mind when *you* were created in your mother's womb. His goal is to have a forever, non-stop loving relationship with you! And that is what is being implied by the word *sin* in the Bible. That is how far Satan has corrupted the word's meaning in our mind. Satan wants us to immediately become fearful and go into hiding and become disconnected from the relationship God wants with us. That is why Satan has driven the word *sin* to be connected to condemnation, fear, and God's anger. Satan always does anything and everything he can to blind us to the love of God (See 2 Corinthians 4:4). Satan wants us to fear a disapproving God instead of being drawn to a loving God.

Could this be why:

- Some people don't read the Bible. Could they be afraid that they will feel condemned?
- Some people don't go to church. Are they afraid they will feel condemned?
- Some people don't want to talk about God or Jesus. Are they afraid they will feel condemned?
- And on and on . . .

Please read and reread this: Not once, no, not once, has Jesus Christ or his Father, ever looked at you in disgust! Never, ever! In the midst of your worst sin, Jesus looks at you with only sadness that you are going in a direction away from him and all the love and good things he wants to do for you and give to you are now in jeopardy. His heart breaks over the potential loss of you! He died so you wouldn't ever have to live in condemnation. The choice is yours.

> *For God did not send his Son into the world to condemn the world, but to save the world through him.* (John 3:17, NIV)

> *Therefore, there is now no condemnation for those who are in Christ Jesus,* (Romans 8:1, NIV)

Rethinking Your Response to Sin

No More Hiding for Me

Failures, weaknesses, and mistakes pushed me into hiding.
Unknowingly as to why, I felt inferior and became a victim of Satan's lying.

To believe the most important person in the universe wanted a relationship with me,
was something totally impossible and could never be.

If God wants to meet me, which I didn't believe he does;
I'm not on that list of important people that he admires nor loves.

I have accomplished so very little in this world and made so little difference:
Compared to others, I do not qualify to be on his list of people of importance.

But reading in the book of all books I learned I had it wrong,
the Bible made it clear, I have been deluded all along.

God made me and has had his eyes on me since the day of my birth.
It is NOT my accomplishments, or the lack thereof,
but it is He alone who will give me my worth!
He alone will remove the stain and soil of all my sin,
and He alone will provide a relationship bridge back to him.

Forgiveness is the enormous gift that he offered me,
When He wrongly, but willingly died on Calvary's tree,
and from the curse of shame and hiding, he has now set me free.

No longer will the consequences of my sin, will He condemn,
And what is more, He is coming back for me, and with him, I will ascend!

Part A: Journey Joy Killer Four

My Journal for My Journey

When I realize I have sinned, I feel . . .

This is how I will handle feelings of condemnation . . .

When I see the face of Jesus in my mind, he has a look of . . .

I believe God wants to have an uninterrupted and ongoing relationship with me, and that makes me want to . . .

Part B

Journey Joy Maker Four

Are You Being Pushed or Pulled into Your Days?

Taking Charge of Your Journey

THE SUN COMES UP every day, just as God designed and put in motion in the beginning of time as recorded in Genesis. It happens whether we want it to or not. It is out of our control; and it's just going to continue to happen until the end of time. You can bet on it. I've had those days when I didn't want to see the dawning of a new day, because what I was facing on that particular day was too unpleasant, and I would rather the world would just end or skip over that day. Have you had those days? Other times, the night seemed so long, and I couldn't wait for the sun to come up on the new day. It was because I was excited about what I believed that day was holding for me.

In studying this, I read a survey of 2,000 adults that delved into how people felt when they initially awakened in the morning. They found that a Joy Killing 89% were not motivated to get up. Their conclusion was that for the vast majority of people, waking up can be kind of a drag. Or stated in reverse order, only 11% of people were motivated to get up and begin a new day when they awakened.

These two contrasting moods can be defined as:

- I'm being pulled (drawn) into another day.
- I'm being pushed into another day.

These are two very different motivations as we inch forward on our journey on a day-by-day basis. It's in our best interest for us to spend a few minutes examining how we are journeying. It will become apparent to you just how much these two forces control the quality of our daily lives as well as our aging process. To a large extent, they are determining the very state of our daily happiness.

To the degree we are able, we can and must accept responsibility for each of these two forces and monitor how they are determining how we are living. It is so easy to fall into a harmful pattern of passive living (Whatever will be, will be.) And when you see a person seemingly trapped in this destructive rhythm, you wish you could somehow just reach in and shake them out of their noxious routine. We want so badly to wake them up so they can see the self-inflicted damage they are doing to themselves. But all too often, they are habitually living on autopilot. Like so many, they are just going from day to day in their nonstop consumption of a blaring TV, or the deafening noise coming through their earplugs, or glued to the screens of their smart phones.

Please allow me to hit the pause button and momentarily change directions and confess an important personal note. It is precisely here that God has two options at his disposal to break this destructive pattern in our lives. He can inject or allow suffering (a reproof) to come into our lives and/or, if we are in relationship with him, He will lead us (an instruction) into deciding to implement a dramatic shift in how we are living. See how he implements it in this verse.

> *He that refuseth instruction despiseth his own soul: but he that heareth reproof getteth understanding.* (Prov 15:32, KJV)

For me, it was both. First, the suffering (reproof) delivered a much-needed wakeup call, followed by his leading (instruction) from answering my repentant prayers. He led this broken-hearted guy into making some much-required changes. I went on a noise fast. I got rid of my TV and ear plugs and went on long walks in the woods. I filled my life with quietness, enabling God and I to start having some of the sweetest and most meaningful and most personal times ever.

> *Be still and know that I am God.* (Ps 46:10 a, KJV)

I can share with you that my previous book (*Untangling the Seven Desires of Your Heart*) and this book you are now reading would not be a reality had God not delivered that double knock-out wake-up call to this thick-headed, stubborn guy. I will forever and ever be grateful to him.)

Okay, let's get back on the subject on hand, how can we proactively manage these two very contrasting forces that govern our daily happiness. Let's take them one at a time.

I'm being pushed into another day:

This is often an individual who is being asked to advance another person's agenda or has been given the responsibility to accomplish a project for someone. It can also include an unpleasant chore or event which is scheduled for tomorrow. The revealing and important element is what's the underlying motive for accomplishing the obligations for that day?

If it involves doing something you don't like, or for a person you don't like, then you are being pushed into your next day. You are beginning your day as a victim because you would rather be somewhere else doing something else and for someone else. Starting your day as a victim is always going to rob you of happiness and a sense of daily meaningfulness. Once you recognize your victim feeling, you can then do something about it. You must resolve that you will not allow yourself to live in the role of a victim, not ever!

The only way I've been able to stay free of victimhood is to start my day while my head is still on my pillow and repeating and applying this verse: *And whatever you do, whether in word or deed, do it all in the name of the Lord Jesus, giving thanks to God the Father through him.* (Col 3:17, (NIV) When I choose to do whatever my day holds for Jesus, I immediately free myself from being a victim of anyone else. If I cannot do it for him, then I shouldn't be doing it. It makes decision making easy and most importantly, I avoid being pushed into another day!

I'm being pulled (Drawn) into another day:

This Joy Making attitude changes things dramatically. Because of what you are doing and for whom you are doing it, you are excited about getting up and getting at it. You have a natural energy and people around you find your excitement contagious. More importantly, you are having a happy day!

There is, however, a warning that needs to be stated. If you are not doing what you are doing in the name of Jesus or for Jesus, and you didn't have that pillow prayer talk before you got out of bed, you may be involved in idol chasing and are having a narcissistic lifestyle day. Its lure can pull you out of bed and into your day in order to achieve another false high. The Bible gives a stern warning against this type of idol chasing:

Part B: Journey Joy Maker Four

For you have spent enough time in the past doing what pagans choose to do—living in debauchery, lust, drunkenness, orgies, carousing and detestable idolatry. (1 Pet 4:3, NIV)

I'm being drawn forward by Jesus: There is the one ultimate force and motivation that is available to us as Christians as we get out of bed every morning; it is the best of all forces and motivations. It's simply Jesus. He says it this way:

"And I, if I be lifted up from the earth, will draw all men unto me." (John 12:32, KJV)

Better than being pushed and selfishly pulled, there is a potential and superior motivation that is only available to us as Christians. We can be drawn (think enticed, lured, loved) into our day, we can and will be drawn forward. When we love someone, we hunger to be with them. It's is not about what we are doing, it is all about who we are doing it with and for! And as we discover our own personal ways of lifting Christ up in our thinking (Bible reading, worship, prayer, meditation etc.) per his promise, he will always draw us forward to himself. If there is such a thing as a secret to living, surely this is it. When in our day we are mindful of getting closer and closer to Jesus, we can march through hell to be with him. And when we are journeying under these conditions, we are in fact, traveling joyfully!

Rethinking Your Response to Sin

Pushed or Pulled

Some days seem so very long and dreary.
My energy is low as my mind becomes weary.

I've come to realize it's when I'm allowing myself to become a victim of pushing.
It's when I'm experiencing that unwelcome outside-in pressuring.

I've given up control to an outside negative directive.
When I live under these conditions, I'm much less effective.

But God offers us a choice, we can change who it is that we're serving,
We can change our allegiance to someone that is so much more deserving.

We can replace the person in our mind to our Lord Jesus,
and in the moment that we make that shift, he immediately frees us.

Now we can do whatever we do, all to the glory of God.
Instead of stewing in self-pity, we can live in a state of being awed.

There is only room in our hearts for one lord and master.
With Jesus as our Lord, our days fly by much faster.

He pulls us forward in the direction of heaven, our eternal dwelling place,
enabling us to travel through difficult times at a much faster pace.
Pull me forward Lord Jesus, close the distance between you and me.
From earthly toil, set me free
until I can be forever with thee.

Part B: Journey Joy Maker Four

My Journal for My Journey

I have some pushers in my life. They include . . .

I enjoy the excitement of being pulled into another day when . . .

This is how I can do an unpleasant job to the glory of God . . .

Working only for Jesus instead of man frees me from . . .

5

Allowing God's Love to Determine Your Self-Esteem

THIS CHAPTER IS GOING to challenge your view of yourself. Probably, nowhere else is the difference between today's popular psychological approach and God's approach more apparent than on the subject as to how to build and sustain a healthy and strong self-identity (self-image plus self-esteem). My interest in this subject began several years ago when I manned a suicide prevention line. And with the out-of-control escalation rates of suicide, this must be one of the top concerns for those of us that are Christ followers. Part A will challenge the world's thinking in this life and death area. Then in a total change of direction, Part B will take you down a very different path. I promise you that you will breathe fresh air and feel the calmness of nature's best messages. You will come away being both refreshed and loved. This is one of the greatest underleveraged joy makers.

In his loving and mighty grip,

LaVon

Part A

Journey Joy Killer Five

Is Your Self-Identity Slowly Killing You?

From Where Did Your Self-Identity Come, and Where Is It Taking You?

WHEN THE PARTY IS over and the music dies down, when the people have all gone home and when you are once again all alone in the darkness, when you look into that wonderful and equally terrifying place called you, with no judgment, just raw honesty, what defines you? What tells you who you are? Is it your looks? Is it your past or your present? Is it everything that everybody ever did to hurt you? Is it the approval and applause of the people currently in your life? Is it your education? Marriage or lack thereof? Your job? Is it the girl or boy you loved so much that broke your heart, stepped on it, ground it in the dust, threw the pieces to the wind, and then turned their back on you and walked away? What is it? Who are you? And what defines you? From where does your self-identity come?

In this chapter, let's have a good and honest talk about you. Let's ask and answer this most important question about you. You have in your mind a self-identity; how did it get there? Did you think and pray about it and then carefully created a you-specific identity, and then purposely set your internal navigation GPS to achieve it? Or did your self-identity just somehow end up there on its own? Have you thought about how much power and influence your self-identity has over you and your life? Or its influence on how you feel about yourself? Are you living with a monster, capable of making a total mess out of your life, or a friend, capable of guiding you to become a godly role model for many to follow?

Allowing God's Love to Determine Your Self-Esteem

As we delve into this vital question regarding your personal self-identity, please notice this chapter is under the heading of journey joy killer, not journey joy maker. The reason for that is that most people have never evaluated or chosen their own self-identity, nor did they even know they could or should accept responsibility as to what it is. Have they considered the enormous influence their self-identity has on their disposition of life? Did they know that by choosing and correcting their self-identity, they have the power of setting themselves free from unwanted habits and addictions to become a whole new and different person, and as a result they could be making very different decisions about their life and how to live it? Our self-identity affects how we make judgments and reach conclusions as to how to behave. But strong negative self-identities can also be extremely dangerous and self-defeating. The drive to protect your identity can be overpowering. Sometimes we can get so caught up in this that we neglect other important things: like being open-minded, truth-seeking, and kind to others.

Jesus told the parable of the Good Samaritan to show us the hideous lack of compassion caused by a weak and inflated self-identity. A traveler was attacked and beaten by robbers and left for dead. He was passed by both by a priest and a Levite. Their self-identities as religious persons put them into an elitist category which didn't have time to show love and compassion for the lowlifes. In a stark contrast, a Samaritan (considered part of the lowest class of people), who also traveled on the same road saw the robbed and beaten victim and immediately and without hesitation assisted by compassionately taking him into the village and paying for his care. Jesus used this most unlikely person, a Samaritan, to illustrate how one's loving servant type of self-identity responded with game-changing love (Luke 10:25–37). It's a real and fair question that Jesus is posing. What would your self-identity cause you to do in that same situation? He wants us to think about that, that is why he told the parable. So, let's honor him and talk about it.

Perhaps even more of an insight into the power and impact of our self-identity is the role Adam and Eve's self-identity played in the original sin. Read this biblical account found in Genesis 3 and see if you can figure out how Satan toyed with Eve's self-identity:

> He (Satan) *said to the woman, "Did God actually say, 'You shall not eat of any tree in the garden'?" And the woman said to the serpent, "We may eat of the fruit of the trees in the garden, but God said, 'You shall not eat of the fruit of the tree that is in the midst of the garden,*

> neither shall you touch it, lest you die.'" But the serpent said to the woman, "You will not surely die. For God knows that when you eat of it your eyes will be opened, and you will be like God, knowing good and evil." (Gen 3:1b-5, ESV)

Note that before Eve sinned by eating the forbidden fruit, her self-identity of being a loved child of God with complete and total trust in God's loving provision and best intentions for her had to be changed. Satan cleverly changed her identity into one of becoming a victim who was being mistreated and lied to by God. Until her pure self-identity was transformed into a victim self-identity, she would not have sinned. After her self-identity was changed to that of a victim, she then felt entitled to the forbidden fruit and free to sin by eating it. This graphically shows that an erroneous victim self-identity influenced by Satan and his minions is a prerequisite of sinning. It also establishes Satan's role in influencing our personal thinking about ourselves, which affects our self-identities. (More on how our self-identities can be strengthened later in this chapter.)

Narrow or elitist self-identities in the minds of national and political leaders are the cause of racism, bigotry, wars, deplorable class systems, and on and on and on. To say that many of humanity's evil and horrendous events are the bad outcomes caused by faulty self-identities of people who have power is a gross understatement. If you haven't concluded it yet, please reach this conclusion now; your self-identity is really a very big deal!

Given its massive potential for having a huge impact on your life for both good and evil, let's begin anchoring this critical conversation by identifying some of these foundational basics.

First allow me to quickly say, whereas all these things mentioned above and below can certainly play a key role in your self-identity, but then again, they may not. There are many people who are not paying attention to life and are just drifting through life on autopilot. Others are reactively ending up with a self-concept based on the experiences I am cataloging. But by contrast, and much more importantly, still others proactively and prayerfully create their self-identity with God's guidance. It is this last category I'm wanting you to consider joining for your personal benefit and God's glory!

How most people define themselves:

It is always simplest to look at ourselves superficially and see what is perfect or acceptable about us or what isn't at first glance. We can judge ourselves based on how many friends we have calling our phone, the likes

Allowing God's Love to Determine Your Self-Esteem

on Facebook®, the love on Instagram®, the invitations to the best parties in town. We define ourselves by how we look in the mirror. We define ourselves by our deeds. We define ourselves by how we think other people would like to see us. We define ourselves according to what would get the most approval and not rock the boat of other people's comfort zones, which might be labeled as hate speech. We define and redefine ourselves by so many different measures and standards of what is considered conventional and natural, but really, what defines you? Often one ends up with a confused self-identity which is like having no identity at all. And without an identity, wherever you end up in life will have to be acceptable.

Or might it just be the relationships that didn't last but taught you hurtful lessons that will make you better in the long run? Is it the appreciation of the random act of kindness from a total stranger? Is it the hope you feel that, regardless of whatever is happening in your life now, that might seem like more than anyone should bear, you want to believe that you will be okay? Is it the smile of your baby that equally fills you up and drains you because you never knew love could feel so pure? Is it the tragedies in your life that have molded and scarred you, making you more compassionate to human suffering or, did it turn you in the exact opposite direction and you became a bitter victim oozing with self-pity? So really, how did you arrive at your self-identity?

Instead of fixating on things that are often out of your control, please think about changing from a reactive approach to a proactive approach for creating your self-identity. No matter how tough the cards we're dealt, what matters most is how we chose to play them.

What does God have to say about all of this?

How our self-identity is formed is of grave concern to God. He does not want us to just end up reactively with a self-identity that represents the summation of all our experiences. There is a much better way; He wants to guide us in choosing our self-identity. He says it this way:

> *Do not be conformed to this world but be transformed by the renewal of your mind, that by testing you may discern what is the will of God, what is good and acceptable and perfect.* (Rom 12:2, ESV)

Notice how he infers that the world is actively conforming (think molding) us to its worldview that is filled with corrupt thinking and godless rebellion philosophies, all of which are bad for us. He plainly states that he wants our self-identity to reflect his will for our lives., which is good for us. He tells us that our mind, the home of our self-identity, must be *transformed* and he describes as becoming *perfect*. He calls on us to test our self-identity to discern that is *acceptable* to him. If you didn't think your self-identity was a big deal before, you can now see it's a big deal to God. So how do we fulfill this demand and create our self-identity that glorifies God and maximizes who we were designed to be? You will now see that it is not only fun, but it is the most liberating and exhilarating experience you can possibly have. It is the key for having a joyful journey through life, regardless of what happens and how bad it is or was.

As an aside thought, in preparing to write this chapter, I researched what many of the psychology experts and their journals were saying about self-esteem, self-identity, self-image, and self-worth, and it made me somewhat disheartened. Their answer to our self-identity crises in our modern times is not working, it is not decreasing the escalating suicide death rates, drug and alcohol addiction rates, marriage crisis rates, etc. It is so pathetically demoralizing to read their shallow solutions to the self-identity crises epidemic plaguing our land. We, of all people, are so blessed to have been given by God an astonishing and an authoritative prescription in his Word (Bible). If you haven't thought about this subject before, it is most likely going to blow your mind! Both its simplicity and power are absolutely amazing.

Formal definition of self-identity: Our self-identity, which defines who we are and who we are becoming, is an overlapping composite of two components, our self-image combined with our self-esteem (sometimes called self-worth). Together, they create our self-identity. Think of it as an algorithm like this: self-image plus self-esteem equals self-identity.

To make this enormous problem of weak and confused self-identities that are stalking and ruining people's lives, we need a solution that is simple to understand and simple to implement. I've found it helpful to put it into two, easy foundational steps to apply. They echo what God says about you. To build a powerful self-identity, you will need to believe that you are who God says you are. Let's take them one at a time.

Step One: Adopt the view that God has of you (your self-image).

First, an important warning: your current self-image may not necessarily reflect reality, so it should not be trusted. That is why God says in Romans 12:2, the Scripture we looked at previously, says it must be tested. But tested how, or by what? Read on. A person with anorexia who is thin may have a self-image in which the person believes they are fat. A person's self-image is affected by many factors and illusions (or delusions), such as overly negative parental influences who devastated their self-image, or

Allowing God's Love to Determine Your Self-Esteem

overly positive parental influences, who falsely inflated their ego. For you, was it some of your compliant friends, or maybe even your loud and vocal enemies? Or your self-image may reflect your guilty conscience of something shameful in your past that has never been resolved and forgiven. Or your thinking may be contaminated by the distorted world views of media, movies, and the music to which you are routinely listening.

This list can become very long. But be it understood that if your self-image is based on any of these kinds of influences mentioned above, you are in jeopardy of living an imaginary life, and unconsciously living a lie. That is why your first and foremost responsibility to yourself is to agree with God that what he says you are is exactly the same as what *you* say you are. You must at some point make a rock-solid decision to say, "I am who God says I am!" Nothing else can be or should be trusted. Your life is much too important to you and to God to risk it on anything else. Don't cheat or betray yourself! Here is an abbreviated and authoritative list of seven dependable and foundational truths to jumpstart your thinking about the groundwork on which your self-image should rely: (This exclusive list is only for those of you who have received Jesus as both Lord and Savior of your lives. All others are encouraged to consider accepting the love Jesus offers to you and become born again under his lordship before reading further. This will then enable these liberating truths to be describing you.)

- I am a child of God! *But to all who did receive him, who believed in his name, he gave the right to become children of God.* (John 1:12, ESV)
- As a child of God, I am a fellow heir of Christ. *And if children, also heirs—heirs of God and coheirs with Christ—if indeed we suffer with him so that we may also be glorified with him.* (Rom 8:17, CSB)
- I am a friend of Jesus, who is Lord of lords and King of kings. *No longer do I call you servants, for the servant does not know what his master is doing; but I have called you friends, for all that I have heard from my Father I have made known to you.* (John 15:15, ESV)
- I will not be and am not now condemned by God! *There is therefore now no condemnation for those who are in Christ Jesus.* (Rom 8:1, ESV)
- I am daily becoming a new and better person in Christ. *So then, if anyone is in Christ, he is a new creation. The old has passed away. The new has come!* (2 Cor 5:17, EHV)

Part A: Journey Joy Killer Five

- I am God's personal workmanship equipped to do good things. *For we are his workmanship, having been created in Christ Jesus for good works, which God has before prepared that we should walk in them.* Eph 2:10, DARBY)

- I have dignity and value because I am fearfully and wonderfully made in the very image of God. *So God created man in his own image, in the image of God e created him; male and female he created them.* (Gen 1:27, NKJV)

Either you believe what God says about you or you don't. I double dare you to compare what he says about you as a Christian to that of any other person, any religion, any worldly authority, any so-called expert, and you will very quickly see the huge difference, and you will want to settle for nothing less than the best. Nowhere are such wonderful, redeeming, liberating, present, and future benefits ever said to us and about us. Really, it just doesn't get any better than this. As a Christ-follower, this is who you are! Read them, memorize them, repeat them over and over, again and again.

If needed. say them so loudly to yourself that they drown out any negative things anybody anywhere is saying about you or to you. Over and over again, repeat them to yourself until your own self-doubts are smothered into stillness and all that remains are these pure, tender, and loving words that God says about you and about who you are.

These truths must be the core of your self-image. Yes, you can add other personal descriptions on top of these seven truths, but they must all be congruent with what God is saying about you. You must never, ever allow yourself to become emotionally, intellectually, or spiritually disconnected from these foundational truths that determine who you are and who you are becoming. To do so would make you just another floundering idiot tossed about by the tormenting winds of people's opinions and philosophies. Daily, you would be on an emotional roller coaster headed nowhere. And that, my dear friend, is not a life that you want to experience! You want to be living in these truths and you want your self-image to be built on this rock-solid foundation. This is deserving of 100 percent of your attention as to how you define yourself. Again, you are who God says you are. And always remember, who you think you are is who you are going to end up becoming.

Step Two: Adopt the value God places on you. (Your self-esteem, also sometimes called self-worth)

Allowing God's Love to Determine Your Self-Esteem

Self-esteem refers to the extent to which we like, accept, or approve of ourselves, or how much we value ourselves. When we give the world permission to define this, it always involves a degree of evaluation and we may end up having either a positive or a negative view of ourselves. Predictably, most people end up somewhere under the low self-esteem category. Often, those who consider themselves on the high self-esteem side can be narcissistic, unless they are there because God put them there. When you buy in to the world's approach, you will end up on one of sides of this list, depending on who and how the evaluation is made. We will see that there is a God-given way to end up on the left column without any mental trickery. We will get to the how in the paragraphs below. But for now, study this and ascertain where you are currently living.

High Self-Esteem (positive view of yourself and life)	Low Self-Esteem (negative view of yourself and life)
Confidence in own abilities	Lack of confidence in own abilities
Self-acceptance	Want to be or look like someone else
Optimism about the future	Pessimistic about life
Not worrying about what others think	Always worrying what others might think
Victor mentality	Victim mentality
Gratefulness, bursting with appreciation	Wounded and prone to feeling self-pity

God does not leave our self-esteem to chance, it's far too important. He does not want you to be put at risk in a world that will beat you down and be vulnerable to Satan, who wants you to feel unworthy and like a nobody. God gives us a better way to live and a sure way to once and for all solidify our self-esteem, ensuring an indisputable and much coveted high self-worth. This alone radically transforms who we are and how we feel about ourselves. Only through Christ can this be obtained. Therapy can't do it, nor can you in a million years of trying to secure it. Only through Christ can it be obtained without ever having to fear that you can lose it. You did not earn it on your own, therefore you cannot lose it on your own.

Part A: Journey Joy Killer Five

No more living on an emotional roller coaster. No more wondering if you are important or have a special purpose in life. And you will have it when God says you have it; listen to him say it to you now: Again, these amazing truths are only for those of you who have claimed Jesus Christ as your personal Lord and Savior.

- The God of the universe, who loves me, has chosen me to be part of his royal family forever. *We know, brothers and sisters loved by God, that he has chosen you.* (1 Thess 1:4, (NIV)

- My adoring God sings love songs over me. *The LORD your God is with you, the Mighty Warrior who saves. He will take great delight in you; in His love He will no longer rebuke you but will rejoice over you with singing.* (Zeph 3:17, NIV)

- I am a certified citizen of heaven. *But our citizenship is in heaven. And we eagerly await a savior from there, the Lord Jesus Christ.* (Phil 3:20, NIV) In Christ Jesus, I have wisdom, righteousness, sanctification, and redemption.

- *He is the reason you have a relationship with Christ Jesus, who became for us wisdom from God, and righteousness and sanctification and redemption.*(1 Cor 1:30, NET) God has given me a reason and purpose for my existence at this time in human history. *"For I know the plans I have for you," declares the LORD, "plans to prosper you and not to harm you, plans to give you hope and a future."* (Jeremiah 29:11. NIV)

When you are who God says you are, then these five truths above are descriptions of you and your high self-esteem and high self-worth. Never doubt them or question them. In Christ, this is who you are. As you look at the matrix that I included several paragraphs above, you can now put your finger on each point in the left hand column and know and thank God that this is now describing you; you can have confidence in this if you believe you are who God says you are! Amazing, I so wish every hurting individual, every person experiencing low self-esteem in the world, could hear and see these truths and come to this belief in order to feel the way this simple matrix promises and allows you to feel about yourself.

The greatest bottom line in the world: (The grand finale of discovering your self-identity)

> *Jesus continued: "There was a man who had two sons. The younger one said to his father, 'Father, give me my share of the estate.' So, he*

Allowing God's Love to Determine Your Self-Esteem

divided his property between them. Not long after that, the younger son got together all he had, set off for a distant country and there squandered his wealth in wild living. After he had spent everything, there was a severe famine in that whole country, and he began to be in need. So, he went and hired himself out to a citizen of that country, who sent him to his fields to feed pigs. He longed to fill his stomach with the pods that the pigs were eating, but no one gave him anything. When he came to his senses, he said, 'How many of my father's hired servants have food to spare, and here I am starving to death! I will set out and go back to my father and say to him: Father, I have sinned against heaven and against you. I am no longer worthy to be called your son; make me like one of your hired servants.' So, he got up and went to his father. "But while he was still a long way off, his father saw him and was filled with compassion for him; he ran to his son, threw his arms around him and kissed him. "The son said to him, 'Father, I have sinned against heaven and against you. I am no longer worthy to be called your son.' "But the father said to his servants, 'Quick! Bring the best robe and put it on him. Put a ring on his finger and sandals on his feet. Bring the fattened calf and kill it. Let's have a feast and celebrate. For this son of mine was dead and is alive again; he was lost and is found.' So, they began to celebrate."
(Luke 15:11–32, NIV)

Why do you think Jesus told this parable? And why did the father run to meet his prodigal son? Why did his father put a ring on his finger, put the best royal robe on him, and sandals on his feet? And why did his father kill the fatted calf and have a great feast? Why did they all stop what they were doing and celebrate? The answer is both profound and simple. Jesus wants us to see how he heals and elevates the prodigal son's severely wounded self-image and repairs his self-esteem (self-worth). The ring, the robe, and the feast where everybody celebrated were targeting a young man's self-image and self-worth which the world had completely destroyed. The young man that was, dirty, smelling like a pig pen, had tattered clothes, was homeless and shoeless, without status, head hanging down, and completely broken. But in a moment, the loving father changed and healed his son's self-identity. Do you get the full picture? Yes, God wants you saved, but he also wants your self-identity (self-perception) healed! God wants you to have a joyful life, and he knows that cannot happen unless you have a healthy self-image and self-esteem—the two components forming a strong self-identity! It's not just about saving you and getting you to heaven; he wants to restore your self-identity in the here and now. If you give him permission to own

Part A: Journey Joy Killer Five

your self-identity, he will heal and elevate it out of love, and he will impart his own status to your status. (It's called godliness.) Have you accepted it? Are you who God says you are? And your answer is: _____.

Allowing God's Love to Determine Your Self-Esteem

From a Nobody to a Somebody

Often when alone, in the darkness and quietness of the night,
I wonder if I'm relevant. Will I have made a difference? That is my fright.
Will the world be a better place because I was here?
Will I leave more love and light behind after I disappear?
I want to be remembered for more than just having passed through,
I want Jesus to be better known, with more love and adoration to him be due.
But I am so weak, so powerless, and so inconsequential.
Only Jesus can use a nobody, it's his love and power that are essential.
He alone must become my identity,
he alone can use me successfully.
He alone can make me a somebody who can make a difference,
he will use me for another lonely or hurting person's deliverance.
Oh, precious Jesus, you give me my self-worth,
you met me where I was and gave me a spiritual rebirth.
Now I'm being remade into your loving image,
to become more like you is now my privilege.
You have canceled and elevated my low self-esteem,
by giving me citizenship in heaven, my forever dream.

Thank you, Jesus!

Part A: Journey Joy Killer Five

My Journal for My Journey

Sometimes my self-image is weak, and it makes me feel like . . .

Here is why I have had problems with self-worth, I . . .

After this study, I'm going to . . .

I believe God wants me to think and pray about these heartfelt concepts discussed in this section . . .

Part B

Journey Joy Maker Five

Are You Benefiting from Both Revelations?

Opting Outside

It is important to understand that we cannot know anything about God unless he reveals himself to us. God is infinite, and we are finite. The distance between God and man is so great that we could not know anything about him, including, what he had in mind for us when he brought each of us into existence, or his unbelievable love for each of us if he did not reveal is thoughts and plans for each of us. Without these revelations, we would be totally lost and confused, without hope, floundering in our ignorance. As Isaiah says, *For as the heavens are higher than the earth, so are my ways higher than your ways and my thoughts than your thoughts.*(Isa 55:9, ESV) Thank God that he communicates his thoughts to all of us who are willing to listen!

There are two ways that God reveals himself to us. Theologians classify these as special and natural revelation. Special revelation is when God speaks to us in his Word, the Bible. It is in the scared Scriptures that God speaks to us authoritatively. It is called *special* in that it is clear and direct in its guidance on how we can take full advantage of God's amazing love. The Bible is unlike *natural* revelation, which is general in nature, implying it is open to everyone who goes outside and will look, listen, and think while viewing all that nature has to offer them. Natural revelation offers no specific direction or life guidance instructions. It simply displays and proclaims a magnificent and all-powerful God who daily showers us with unbelievable beauty. We will document nature's specific messages later in this chapter.

Both revelations (specific and natural) are essential if we are to have a complete understanding of both God's love and our individual life's potential. Knowing when we need to read and dwell in each revelation is vital if we are to take full advantage of God's communications to us. It is the purpose of this chapter to bring God's speaking through these two communication channels into balance so each of us can hear and receive God's loving and nudging whispers guiding us forward, as well as God's shouts and cries of power in which to trust and take refuge. One thing will become abundantly clear, God is talking to us! Are we listening?

Having respect and reverence for both revelations begins with this immutable principle: All truth is God's truth: He is the originator and owner of all truth. Truth that he delivers through the Bible is infallible, and truth he delivers through nature is equally infallible. And because of this, Satan has no other alternative but to attempt to distort and discredit the truth in both revelations in order to infuse doubt into people's minds, blinding them to the glory of Christ (2 Cor. 4:4). It is not my purpose in this chapter to provide a complete apologetical defense of both specific revelation (the Bible) or natural revelation (man's environment, earth, and universe). But we can be affirmed when we ask, "What is true?" This question is often presented as a deep philosophical puzzle suitable only for the brainy to tackle, but the answer is not so complex. It is just a matter of common sense. Truth is what corresponds to reality. Consequently, what is real is true, what is unreal is false. Let's take a quick second to appeal to your common sense as you look at reality in both revelations:

1. The infallibility of the Bible's revelation:

    For thousands of years people have cast accusation after accusation against the Bible, and every accusation has been answered and proven wrong. (Numerous books are available in this area.) But as a matter of simple common sense, our Bible is composed of sixty-six books by forty different writers over 1500 years. The astounding thing about this is that the Bible is completely unified around both the predictions and their fulfillment in the person of Jesus Christ. How could that have happened if it were not for the divine, guiding hand of God? The historical accuracy of the Bible is continuously verified by every new archeological finding. In short, The Holy Bible is without peer, and common sense alone invites you to bet your eternity on it.

2. The infallibility of nature's revelation:

    Whether you are looking through a telescope or a microscope, it takes only a few seconds to see a visible and intelligent design behind the seasons, the circling planets, and the cycle of life, whether it is from bees and birds of the air or, to worms and bacteria in the soil that produces the abundance of food we eat daily. This leads us to conclude that there is order and design behind God's creation. God's creation works predictively and is therefore dependable. To buy into the notion that we live in on a randomized planet is as foolish as expecting to throw a handful of metal pieces into the air and expect them to come down as a Rolex® watch. Intelligent design demands a designer, and the unquestionable design in nature points to our intelligent God. Common sense alone invites you to bet your eternity on it.

God is speaking. What does he want us to hear when we opt to go outside into nature? (The other chapters in this book are dedicated to the hearing and understanding of what God is saying in the Bible. This chapter is dedicated to hearing and understanding what God is saying through nature.)

Below are two key Scriptures that inform us of why and how we can derive wisdom from natural revelation by opting to go outside. Read them, then we will discuss how taking a midday walk in the woods or a nighttime walk under the night sky can have a great impact on your personal joyfulness as a journey joy maker.

> *The heavens declare the glory of God, and the sky above proclaims his handiwork. Day to day pours out speech, and night to night reveals knowledge.* (Ps 19:1–2 ESV)

> *For what can be known about God is plain to them, because God has shown it to them. For his invisible attributes, namely, his eternal power and divine nature, have been clearly perceived, ever since the creation of the world, in the things that have been made. So they are without excuse.* (Rom 1:19–20, ESV)

The brilliance of God's design in having two separate revelations (Bible and nature) that complement and support each other can be seen and understood by identifying the different role of each revelation:

Natural revelation provides the skeleton or, the foundational framework.

Biblical revelation provides the spiritual meat and muscle on the bones of the skeleton, or the siding and roofing of a home built on the framework.

Part B: Journey Joy Maker Five

Together, they build the whole spiritual man or the whole completed home. As you take note of the sequential construction of a person or home (first the skeleton followed by the muscle, or first the framework followed by the home), it becomes apparent that God had a two-step communication approach in revealing himself to us. First he uses natural revelation as he reveals the general big picture of who he is and his very existence, then he uses biblical revelation to reveal the specific details of how we can have a personal and forever relationship with him and how his love makes it all possible.

Here are three main messages revealed by God to a nonbeliever through natural revelation:

- In his grand plan to reveal himself to us, he uses natural revelation as an attention getter. He knows, that unless we are morally on the run and have become a child of darkness, we will be automatically drawn to a God that creates that stunning and beautiful sunrise. We instinctively want to know the designer and creator of those drop-dead gorgeous flowers and magnificent mountains.

- A wonder starter is where we impulsively begin questioning why and who is behind all this splendid creation and its masterful and intelligent design. How did all of this happen? We want to know, and we feel we need to know. And at that moment in time when wonderment begins, our personal spiritual journey has just started. And God's stated purpose of natural revelation is succeeding for that open-minded and humble questioner.

- When we sit or lay back on the grass on a bright, starry night, gazing up into the endless heavens, we experience a God detector moment. Our commonsense mind begins to formulate answers to questions such as: How could all of this possibly have happened by itself? There must be someone, perhaps a God, making all of this happen. He must be all powerful. His intelligence must have designed all of this. Then the enquiring mind of that observant person goes one step further. Why did he do all of this? Did he also create me? If so, why? How can I get to know him and get answers to my questions of why and how?

It is at this exact point that biblical revelation picks up where natural revelation leaves off and begins to provide answers to the curiosity and inquisitiveness spawned by the natural revelation in our minds. This enables God's promise to be activated.

Allowing God's Love to Determine Your Self-Esteem

Draw near to God, and he will draw near to you. (Jas 4:8a, ESV)

Immediately God goes to work and will providentially provide an angel, or somebody, or a truth that allows that person to decide about taking their next step towards God. This is why the Scripture in Romans says we are without excuse, because God's natural revelation sends a loud and clear message that there is a God who is trying to get in touch with us. And it is how we respond to his natural revelation that will become the basis of how we will be judged on that great and final day when we all stand before the God of the universe.

But for us who are already believers, Christ-followers, and are ongoing students of the biblical revelation, natural revelation still plays a vital but different role. Below are few of God's inspirations waiting for us when we go outside and listen for the messages that come from natural revelation: (Allow me to clarify something in case you reach a wrong and limiting conclusion. It is best by far if you can arrange to go out into nature in person, This will enable you to feel and see the rustling leaves moved by the gentle breeze, and hear the singing birds or babbling brook, or become visually captivated by the pristine beauty of the surrounding creation. But sometimes going out into the natural environment may not be possible. But even then, you can look at pictures, films, or just view nature through a car window. Or you may find yourself starring at a vase of beautiful flowers sitting on the kitchen table. Something, anything, that can deliver to your eyes the natural revelation is better than nothing at all. Be sure to include music, which is also a medium through which natural revelation can often flow. Your eyes and ears are also God's intended receivers of his natural revelation. Anyone who has ever been in a concert hall listening to soothing music of an orchestra with eyes closed and feeling the unbridled and relaxing strains of melodies and harmonies, all blended together, can attest to having had a spiritual experience.

That being said, here is what can happen when you avail yourself of God's natural revelation.

- When our eyes are glued to the giant explosion of colors surrounding a sunset, we cannot help but be compelled to worship as we find ourselves in a natural outdoor cathedral, complete with real-life decorative colors, like stained glass windows. Surrounded by his creation's beauty, we cannot be quiet, but must praise and worship him. With each passing moment of the evolving sunset, we find ourselves cheering God on in celebration.

- In the middle of a woods surrounded by mighty oaks, or watching a volcano spew fire, or hearing the loud, rolling thunder, we are strengthened and inspired by the power of our personal, omnipotent, and protective God.
- Watching the fluttering butterfly or listening to the singing sparrow, we realize God's eyes are on each of us. As he observes the sparrows and as he cares for them, we are also watched over and cared for by him.
- As we are surrounded by flowers or smell the sweetness of the new meadow grasses, we feel loved and cherished due to all the grandeur with which God surrounds us for our enjoyment and pleasure.
- And as the night advances, and barnyard animals retire to the barn to lie down on the straw, and the crickets announce the beginning of night with their chirping, and the stars begin their nightly glow, we feel the relaxing peace coming upon us as we lie down for a good night's sleep, knowing we have a God that doesn't sleep.

He's calling for you! Where are you?

> *And they heard the sound of the LORD God walking in the garden in the cool of the day, and the man and his wife hid themselves from the presence of the LORD God among the trees of the garden. But the LORD God called to the man and said to him, "Where are you?"* (Gen 3:8–9, ESV)

God wants time with you. But to make it meaningful and uninterrupted, he wants some alone time with you. That means you need to go to him on his earthly home turf, away from your home, your job, your car, your busyness, etc. And as it was in the beginning of time in the Garden of Eden, where it was God's greatest delight to walk in his created nature with Adam and Eve in the cool of the day, God wants to meet you in his natural home surrounded by his stuff, his creation. When you leave your stuff behind and join him there, you can have some of the most wonderful and purest talks with God that you've ever had. You will hear and feel things there that cannot be heard or felt anyplace else. He will show you things there that cannot be seen anywhere else. Your mind will reach conclusions there that cannot be reached anywhere else. God wants to be your closest friend, but that cannot happen if you don't spend time together alone

Allowing God's Love to Determine Your Self-Esteem

in his home—in his creation, making new memories and new and deeper relationship experiences.

But on this particular day in the Garden of Eden, Adam and Eve were a no-show. They had gone into hiding because they had let unforgiven sin come between themselves and God. They had let sin destroy the most important relationship known to man with the most important person—God. They hid in shame from the only person who could and wanted to forgive their sinful mistake. Satan had succeeded in getting them to run from the very person who loved them most and who was the only solution to their sinful shame. Satan had momentarily won; he had disconnected them from their God. This is also Satan's goal for you and me. He cannot afford for us to meet God in the woods, he fears we will hear all those life-changing and inspirational messages identified above.

But even as Adam and Eve were hiding, our grace-giving and loving God still came and still called for them as he does with us. God, who is sometimes called the Hound of Heaven, endlessly pursues us up to the very end of our breath. Not to have a forever, loving relationship with us is not only a waste of all the pain and agony he experienced because of Calvary, but also causes God to have sorrow over missing that personal one-on-one relationship with us for which we were created. He treasures time with us!

In conclusion, out in nature right now, God is waiting for you to join him. And as with Adam and Eve, he is pleadingly calling for you to come and spend time with him on his home turf, in nature. He has more truth to give to you, more love to share with you, and more beautiful things he created and wants to show you. He also has that much needed encouragement and inspiration with which to bless and encourage you. When you are a no show, he misses you more than anybody in the world misses you. Nobody can or does love you as much as he does. Run to him in his home, in nature! Do you hear it? As he called Adam and Eve, he is calling: "Where are you?"

Part B: Journey Joy Maker Five

Why?

Have you wondered why the world has so many pretty places?
Have you dreamed of visiting all the different countries and seeing pretty faces?
Have you wondered why God created all
the different kinds of peoples, birds, and animals?
Have you wanted to visit all the different cultures and experience their diverse festivals?
Have you pondered why God made so many kinds of flowers?
Or how he cared for them by providing those gentle rain showers?
And have you been mesmerized by the vastness of the fruited plains,
or the beauty of the golden waves in the fields' bountiful grains?
Have you been awed by the spectacular sight of those mighty snowcapped mountains?
Or those endless, winding rivers with their rainbow laced fountains?
Does it seem like it's all just too much?
To God, it's his way for different people to touch.
For the Bible says that he's not willing that any should perish,
Through each creation component is yet another way a person he can cherish.
So, the reason for all of creation's vastness
is because it enables God's love to touch and heal all the sadness.
Nature is his preferred meeting place for each of us,
a place where all those thorny issues of life, you and God can discuss.
As with Adam and Eve, whom he met in the cool of the day,
he wants likewise to meet with us, for he has something important to say.
He wants you to know that he created all of this for you,
to make it easier during those difficulties of life for you to come through.
And all his creation is his signature invitation saying, "I want more time with you."

Allowing God's Love to Determine Your Self-Esteem

My Journal for My Journey

When you think about having meetings with God on his turf in nature you . . .

How would you describe the balance between natural and biblical revelation in your life?

Please describe a time when you had a meaningful God encounter in nature.

What is it about nature that draws you to it?

6

Understanding God's Way of Managing the People in Your Life

OKAY, I ADMIT IT, somedays I just don't want to see or talk to another person. I get tired of dealing with people. People are messy, and that messiness often spills over into my life and makes my life messier. So, there are times that I just want to get away from all people. My run and hide instincts are not healthy. The truth is, whether I admit it or not, I need people. And I always will. I can't live with them, and I cannot live without them.

God made people, lots of them, all sizes and shapes. And he put me in the center of people. So since he has done this to me, he must have had a way for me to live in the midst of all this humanity, and be happy, and allow them to make me a better person, and use me to work with him to make people in my life better as well.

This chapter is all about people management. It will give you some biblical approaches for living with people. Part A will take you into one of the most severe and dangerous addictions that nobody talks about. And Part B will tell you about a tank that needs to be full if you are ever to get along with people.

Enjoy this people chapter.

LaVon

Part A

Journey Joy Killer Six

The People Pleasing Prison

The Addiction That No One Talks About

IT EVEN HAS ITS own scientific categorized name. It is called allodoxaphobia, and it is the fear of opinions. It is considered a social phobia, a prevalent social anxiety disorder, a mental health condition. It is an intense and persistent fear of being watched and judged by others. It feeds off the need of approval from others to give its victims a higher but false sense of self-esteem. It targets those of us who are convinced that people's recognition matters to our self-worth and determines and impacts how deeply we value ourselves. I know all too well this imprisoning condition, for it has been a life-long personal fight for me. If I had to name the number one thing from which Christ must continually set me free, it's this journey joy killer 6, and it has been by far the number one addiction enemy in my life.

I wrongly thought for years that it was caused by my being the youngest of seven in a poor farm family. All my clothes were hand-me-downs, the worst of which were the old scuffed-up, scraggly shoes I wore to school every day. I allowed my wardrobe to make me self-conscious and drive me into becoming an introvert with low self-esteem. That, along with my lack of social skills from being stuck out in nowhere in a rural setting, seemed to make me a victim due to being dealt a bad hand in life over which I had no control.

That's my story, what's yours? Every one of us has one. Do you believe you are ugly, dumb, can't dance, un-athletic, too tall, not tall enough, can't sing, poor, from the wrong side of the tracks, with a birth mark, overweight, and on and on and on? We all can claim we are a victim in some manner. No one has a cakewalk through life. We all can wish something was different, something that would have given us an edge. So, if we go down this people-pleasing road, none of us will end up as winners, we are all losers in some way. This is a road we should never be on. Any time we compare ourselves to others, we will either win the comparison, which makes us prideful, or we will lose the comparison making us feel like a reject, which is never how God wants us to feel. We lose either way. Just consider these bad outcomes documented in the Bible that happen when we engage in people pleasing:

The worst decision made in all history happened because one key person was a people pleaser.

> *But they shouted louder and louder for Jesus' death, and their voices prevailed. So Pilate sentenced Jesus to die as they demanded.* (Luke 23:23–24, TLB)

Our Lord's death was ordered by Pilate who succumbed to pleasing people as opposed to doing what was true, right, and just. May I say that again? Our Lord was killed by a people pleaser.

Popularity won by people leasing always ends in sadness: *And what sadness is ahead for those praised by the crowds—for false prophets have always been praised.* (Luke 6:26, TLB.) People pleasing popularity is always short-lived and has a disappointing ending.

People pleasers are susceptible to the seducing taunts of evil people: *Don't do as the wicked do. Avoid their haunts—turn away, go somewhere else, for evil men can't sleep until they've done their evil deed for the day. They can't rest unless they cause someone to stumble and fall.* (Proverbs 4:14–16, (TLB.) Misery loves company, evil people will coax you to join them. People pleasers are vulnerable.

People pleasers are defenseless to peer pressure which leads to bad decision making:

> *The king was grieved, but because of his oath, and because he didn't want to back down in front of his guests, he issued the necessary orders.* (Matt 14:9, TLB)

This is how and why the beloved John the Baptist was beheaded by a people pleaser politician wanting to please the public.

Justice is perverted by people pleasing mobs: *Don't join mobs intent on evil. When on the witness stand, don't be swayed in your testimony by the mood of the majority present.* (Exodus 23:2, TLB) Mobs are often composed of people pleasers who have given their allegiance to the loud and powerful.

From this short biblical list above, you can see what everybody intuitively knows. A people pleasing addiction is not only wrong, it leads to bad outcomes. Shakespeare was mistaken, all the world is not a stage; but as a people pleaser, you just think it is. And it is this thought—the belief that you need to perform for an always watching and always critiquing audience—that creates your massive anxiety, pressuring you to conform to the expectations of others. This is impossible to do, because everybody's expectation of you will be different, causing you to be jerked around every which way, resulting in you having a miserable life and leaving you feeling unfulfilled and dissatisfied with living.

So, to alleviate your anxiety and to eliminate the potential of much-feared criticism, you shrink back by becoming dreadfully normal, and you avoid taking risks that could put you in a spotlight. I worst part of doing this is that you end up sacrificing what is so special and unique about you in order to blend in as much as possible. Your addiction causes you to become hesitant to create any waves or ruffle any feathers. This is clearly not the recipe for living your best life for God, who has endowed you with special gifting and special passions and sensitivities designed to help you in hearing his special calling for his own special purpose to be displayed in your life.

> *For I know the plans I have for you, declares the LORD, plans for welfare and not for evil, to give you a future and a hope.* (Jer 29:11, ESV)

You cannot avoid criticism, but you can learn to live with it and not allow it to have such a grip on your life. In other words, you can get to the point where you care so much about what God is doing in and through your life that you become immune to being sidelined by a critical comment, negative review, or raised eyebrow. And when you get to that point, you will have broken out of the people-pleasing addiction and are now free to follow God's guidance in your life and develop and live in the center of your giftedness and passion. That is the way living was met to be. And it doesn't get any better than that!

To get to that point, let's start with some prescriptive reading designed to eradicate people-pleasing addiction from your life. If your case is severe, you will need to take in this truth by reading this on a weekly basis until your symptoms fade away.

Part A: Journey Joy Killer Six

For am I now seeking the approval of man, or of God? Or am I trying to please man? If I were still trying to please man, I would not be a servant of Christ. (Gal 1:10, ESV)

But just as we have been approved by God to be entrusted with the gospel, so we speak, not to please man, but to please God who tests our hearts. (1 Thess 2:4, ESV)

The fear of man lays a snare, but whoever trusts in the LORD is safe. (Prov 29:25, ESV)

Not that we dare to classify or compare ourselves with some of those who are commending themselves. But when they measure themselves by one another and compare themselves with one another, they are without understanding. (2 Cor 10:12, ESV)

And do not fear those who kill the body but cannot kill the soul. Rather fear him who can destroy both soul and body in hell. (Matt 10:28, ESV)

Do not be conformed to this world, but be transformed by the renewal of your mind, that by testing you may discern what is the will of God, what is good and acceptable and perfect. (Rom 12:2, ESV)

And without faith it is impossible to please him, for whoever would draw near to God must believe that he exists and that he rewards those who seek him. (Heb 11:6, ESV)

We stand true to the Lord whether others honor us or despise us, whether they criticize us or commend us. (2 Corinthians 6:8a, TLB)

In applying the truths delineated in the scriptural package of verses you just read, it may help you to group all the causes of people-pleasing addictions into the following two categories:

The Fear of Rejection

As sinful people, we are constantly battling for the need of approval. Because our daily sins produce a guilty conscience (our sins of omission and sins of commission). And since we were created in God's image, our conscience naturally demands holiness or perfection. So, when we sin, we instantly feel separation from God and lose his approval and instantly feel rejection. And like Adam and Eve, we are tempted to go into hiding from God. To make us feel better after losing the approval of God, we try to substitute it with peoples' approval. This triggers the wrong thinking that the more good deeds we do, the more approval we will get, and the better we feel about ourselves, the more loved we will feel. But then we sin again, and we trigger the same chain reaction all over again, perpetuating a never-ending struggle that we can't win.

This is precisely why the gospel means good news. Once we accept his unbelievable offer of salvation which brings total and complete forgiveness because of Jesus having paid the price of every one of our sins, we are given his promise that nothing can ever separate us from the love of God. Are you getting this? We will never, ever be rejected because of our new salvation status given to us by Jesus. That means at this very moment we are 100 percent loved and approved. There is nothing you can ever do that will get you more approval or more love. Salvation settles it, you can take rejection off your worry list. You can celebrate that, and this is why we have worship services, to celebrate his loving approval through Jesus Christ, our Lord and forever Savior.

A vital truth to combat this fear is this: Not everyone will love me, but the one who matters will never stop loving me. God's love for us does not ebb and flow; it does not waver; it does not increase or decrease; it is consistent. Praise God for this fixed truth!

We also don't need to lose our assurance as children of God every time we sin or forget these truths. His love for us is made complete in Christ, so there's no need to fear rejection. Once we are secure in our relationship with God, and understand the implications of that relationship, we will seek to know how we can please him.

When we desire to obey God, the desire to please others fades, and pleasing God becomes more important. Don't try to psych yourself up to the point where you simply don't care enough to let criticism affect you. That strategy is both wrong and dangerous. A much better approach is to care deeply about who you are in Christ and what he is creating and doing in you. Follow your God-given passion and your inspiration. Go where you are called and create what is inside you. Care so much for others that you don't care what they think. This will stop you from seeking approval from others and you will be busy giving to others. The greatest achievements the world has ever seen were started by individuals who marched to the beat of a different drummer. As you set out to impact the world for Christ, just make sure your drum is loud enough to drown out all the critics.

Part A: Journey Joy Killer Six

The Fear of Failure

When people pleasing replaces God pleasing, fear of failure is at the root. People are driven by the need for approval and desire to become successful, not only to avoid being rejected, but for self-approval. Once again, we are focusing on something other than Christ, which is idolatry; we are engaging in people-centered worship and self-centered worship. Many people pleasers believe this kind of behavior is commendable because it involves serving others, but it isn't—it's motivated by approval and the assurance that we are a success. The problem with this is we are often looking to a dark world to define our success instead of looking toward the light of Christ and walking as children of the light:

> *Walk as children of light . . . and try to discern what is pleasing to the Lord.* (Eph 5:8b, 10, ESV)

We go down the wrong road when we attempt to calculate and determine our successfulness. How do you define success? In a biblical story, there was the young lad with five loaves and two fish. Was he successful by offering it to feed 5,000 people? Of course not, it was a dismal failure. But when he placed it in the hands of Jesus, there were baskets of food left over. In man's reality, the boy's solution to the hungry masses was not successful, but when he surrendered it to Jesus, who multiplied it many times over, it was a celebrated success. The boy did not need to feel like a regretful failure. We simply cannot measure God's view of success. What we place in the hands of Jesus will be magnified to do what needs to be done. We should only focus on our heart's motive, not on the world's depiction of our supposed contributions and achievements.

In God's Word we find the truth that can combat this fear. We define success by what brings glory to God. Instead of looking to what we accomplish, how much money we make, who we impressed with our accolades, we simply need to see fruit appearing from our Christ-empowered lives naturally emanating from the relationship we have with Jesus Christ. Our job is to simply prioritize our faithfulness and leave the results up to him. And please reach this all-important conclusion. Our success in Christ cannot and must not be measured. If you try, you will immediately be put back into people-pleasing addiction. If you are trying to measure so you can point to success, you still don't get it. Our job is to *trust and obey, for there is no other way to be happy in Jesus, but to trust and obey*. These words are from an old hymn by the same name, written by John H. Sammis. You have been given the freedom from God to stop letting fear and anxiety prevent you from sharing your God-given creativity, or from being and becoming the person God meant for you to be. God will validate you if or when you need it, and he will encourage you if or when you need it. After all, he is your partner and he will never abandon you, never!

If you have reached a conclusion to break your people-pleasing addiction, please be invited to say this confessional prayer to God the Father.

A People Pleaser's Confessional Prayer

Dear Heavenly Father,

I have been and am most definitely, most unequivocally, most assuredly a people pleaser. Not only have I wanted people to like me, I have wanted them to seek me out for advice and respect. In my weakness, I confess that I have done things to earn approval and have coveted their admiration.

I now hereby accept the truth that I will never be good enough to earn your approval by wrongly attempting to earn the approval of people who are, at the same time, seeking my approval in return. I now only seek *your* approval, and I humbly have given up winning it by my own weak and sinful efforts. I am now an enthusiast of what Christ has already done in my behalf and have gratefully accepted his gracious offer to represent me and his imputed righteousness to me for your approval. He is my Savior, my Lord, and my friend.

Thank you for welcoming me into your kingdom and admitting me into your forever forgiven family. Your love and acceptance are overwhelming, and I find it my pleasure to serve and worship you with all my heart for now and all eternity. My security is totally in you!

Because of Jesus, (your name here)

Part A: Journey Joy Killer Six

Worthless to Worthy

All my sins, along with all my weaknesses, combine to make me unworthy.
In the presence of my holy God, I bow my head in self-pronounced humility.
I so want to be pleasing to God, but I continue to fail at every attempt,
before the sinless judge of the universe, I can only feel contempt.
Having failed with my God, to measure up to earn His approval,
My dream and my invitation to heaven has suffered His removal.
To salvage what's left of my self-esteem, I became a people-pleaser,
trying to earn what they can't give; I continued to become a fulltime seeker.
It became a worsening addiction that I could not beat.
It made the standard that much higher which I could not meet.
Suffering people-pleasing addiction put me in prison with no way out,
then out of desperation, I studied the Bible to learn what Jesus is all about.
In an addiction prison needing people's affirmation for supporting my worthiness,
I learned there was no way to breakout and become free except through Jesus.
His value of me destroys my self-pride, filling me with a love I've never known.
I'm set free by having God's approval as a gift of which before I had never been shown.
Because Jesus is now my Savior,
I have been given his perfection through his unmerited grace.
Now my days are numbered until I will be able to thank him face-to-face.
As a child of the King, a certified member of the family of God,
I'm now worthy to be in his eternal presence, for which I'll be forever awed.

Understanding God's Way of Managing the People in Your Life

My Journal for My Journey

How has thinking about what people think about you impacted you?

Are there things you should be doing but don't because you are afraid of what people may say?

Describe a time when you did something, knowing people would not approve.

I believe God wants me to think and pray about these heartfelt concepts discussed in this section . . .

Part B

Journey Joy Maker Six

Are You Love Ready?

Is Your Love Tank Running on Empty?

THEN GOD SAID, *"LET us make man in our image, after our likeness. And let them have dominion over the fish of the sea and over the birds of the heavens and over the livestock and over all the earth and over every creeping thing that creeps on the earth.* (Gen 1:26, ESV) Notice the words *us* and *our* in the verse above. This denotes a time when God the Father, God the Son, and God the Holy Spirit were having a talk about creating the world and all that is in it. They had just finished making planet earth and its heavens. Now they were ready to finish the creation picture by creating the crown jewel of all creation——humankind. This sparked what I imagine is the following go-or-no-go discussion between the different members of the Holy Trinity about the creation of mankind. This is a pivotal moment in human history, and it necessitated a decisive conversation about the consequences of bringing humanity into existence. This is the likely conversation alluded to in the verse above that they were having. Let's jump into the midst of their holy conversation and notice the all-important ending of their creation discussion. This reconstructed best-guess dialog was happening between verse 26 (above) and verse 27 (below).

God the Father, "We need and are missing a caretaker over all we have created and someone to begin the stewarding and populating of the entire earth."

God the Son, "Yes, someone like us, who can both apply thinking and feeling in their response to each other and to us as their God. It must be

Understanding God's Way of Managing the People in Your Life

someone fully capable of mutual affection, loving respect, and who will accept and execute their stewardship duties with fairness and gladness."

God the Holy Spirit, "Yes, someone who can choose to love us back and with whom we can have a rich and personal ongoing fellowship day-by-day and minute-by minute, someone with a conscience for choosing and doing that which is right in our eyes."

And turning to Jesus, Father-God said, "Son, if we give them free moral volition, they may choose wrong over right and unknowingly become puppets of Satan, resulting in their fate of plunging into hell. Jesus, can you bear the pain and hurt of knowing of that happening to them?"

And God the Son, stepped forward and said, "I will volunteer to intervene in their behalf and pay the full price of their sinful mistakes so they can choose not to be slaves of Satan and escape hell in order to enjoy our friendship forever in heaven and live eternally with the universe as their playground."

Father-God very quickly replied, "But Son, you know that will cost you your heavenly home, and everything you have now, and in return, you will experience every pain and hurt you could ever feel, and every heartache you could ever endure, and every broken dream and expectation from which you could ever grieve, and every shame you could ever know, and the amassed hatred of all mankind aimed at your breaking heart, and the rejection and betrayal of those you love. And on top of all of that, you will die a wicked and unjust death in the cruelest manner. Son, are you absolutely sure you are love ready to risk all of that for all of them who are so undeserving?"

And a severely saddened and sober thinking Son of God, contemplating all the consequences, bowed his head and responded, "Father-God, I am love ready for them and all the sinful mistakes they each will do, let us proceed with their creation. I am ready to pay the price for becoming their forever safety net for all of those who will choose my love over all else. I will do it for the potential of enjoying the sweet bliss of a forever intimate relationship with everyone who chooses to love us in return for our sacrificial love provided to each of them. They will become members of our family, and I will relish them as my brothers and sisters forever and ever."

With the completion of that most holy and determinate conversation, the Bible went on to say: *So God created man in his own image, in the image of God he created him; male and female he created them.* (Gen 1:27, ESV) And that is how we came to be! And in that moment of time, the first appearance of love readiness was seen, and because of its presence, it allowed the creation process to be completed with the creation of Adam and Eve. The beginning of civilization became a reality. And from that point forward, nothing has ever happened for which Jesus was and is not 100 percent love ready. Both that decision and that commitment were irreversibly made and finalized before the final decision to create mankind was implemented. He doesn't ever have to stop and ponder in order to make yet another decision when he sees us turn our backs on him and commit an additional grievous sin. In advance, he already made that hard and painful decision a long time ago. He now, at this very moment, has love readiness for both you and me. By definition, love readiness must be created in advance with each of us, and each hurtful sin we have and will ever commit was already in his mind when he committed to be our personal savior, redeemer, and friend. And when we do sin, as we are prone to do daily to our own disgrace and shame, Jesus has already made that tough decision to cover us with his forgiveness based upon our repentant request, because he is, and always is, 100 percent love ready. We can be assured of this because that forever decision was made way back in the Garden of Eden, enabling mankind to be created. And it was lovingly and thoughtfully made fully knowing that we humans would comment godless, immoral sins, each of which added to the pain and hurt that Christ would have to bear on the cross in our behalf. And knowing all of that, he still made that decision to become love ready for each of us who would humble ourselves and call on his name to be forgiven and saved. Thank God for the love readiness of Jesus Christ!

Now, with that background understanding of that profound and all-encompassing truth, let's turn our attention to each of us and talk about his and our own love readiness. But first, here is a more formal definition.

Definition and explanation of love readiness: We have love readiness when we freely decide to forgive and love people in advance of their mistreatment of us or others that we love. This is based on ourfaith and dependency on Christ to do through us that which he did and is doing to and for us. This is done fully knowing that it may involve unjust pain and unfair embarrassment which allows our love to be even more God glorifying. Without God's powerful love in us, we cannot have or implement love readiness in our own lives. It is our gift of pleasure to allow God to love others through our hearts. There simply is no greater thrill than to experience God's big love flowing through our small hearts! When this happens, we immediately know that's why we're here and this is what we are meant to do. We immediately feel relevant to both God and man. Oh, that we could experience that every day so our lives would be filled with unmatchable meaningfulness. If we have love readiness, God can make that a reality.

The reason we are having this discussion about love readiness is because of these God-given instructions itemized below, and God's life-changing truths that are guiding us in and through his Word. (Read slowly and thoughtfully.)

> *We love because he first loved us.* (1John 4:19, ESV)

> *And so, we know and rely on the love God has for us. God is love. Whoever lives in love lives in God, and God in them.* (1 John 4:16, NIV)

> *Do everything in love.* (1 Cor 16:14, NIV)

> *Be completely humble and gentle; be patient, bearing with one another in love.* (Eph 4:2, NIV)

> *Above all, love each other deeply, because love covers over a multitude of sins.* (1 Pet 4:8, NIV)

> *I pray that out of his glorious riches he may strengthen you with power through his Spirit in your inner being, so that Christ may dwell in your hearts through faith. And I pray that you, being rooted and established in love, may have power, together with all the Lord's holy people, to grasp how wide and long and high and deep is the love of Christ.* (Eph 3:16–18, NIV)

> *My command is this: Love each other as I have loved you.* (John 15:12, NIV)

> *Be devoted to one another in love. Honor one another above yourselves.* (Rom 12:10, NIV)

> *Whoever claims to love God yet hates a brother or sister is a liar. For whoever does not love their brother and sister, whom they have seen, cannot love God, whom they have not seen.* (1 John 4:20, NIV)

> *Greater love has no one than this: to lay down one's life for one's friends.* (John 15:13, NIV)

> *Let all bitterness and wrath and anger and clamor and slander be put away from you, along with all malice. Be kind to one another, tenderhearted, forgiving one another, as God in Christ forgave you.* (Eph 4:31–32, ESV)

Part B: Journey Joy Maker Six

And lead us not into temptation but deliver us from evil. For if you forgive others their trespasses, your heavenly Father will also forgive you. (Matt 6:13–14, ESV)

But to you who are listening I say: Love your enemies, do good to those who hate you. (Luke 6:27, (NIV)

Wow, that is one powerful accumulation of instructive truths! It alone is deserving of its own book, complete with hundreds of footnotes and references. But for the purpose of this chapter, I want you to take away from this abbreviated list of love truths a deep knowing and belief that love is the foundation, the center, and the grand ending of our relationship with God. It is what distinguishes us as being Christ-followers wrapped in divine love, which is vastly different from every religion and every alternative scheme for living. It is the essence of what it means to be a Christian. It is why I choose this subject, for journey joy maker six: love readiness.

We are the recipients of the love readiness of our Lord. That being the case, the next question becomes, how can we become benefactors with our own love readiness to others that God providentially brings into our lives? For when that happens, we will have reached the ultimate succus for achieving the very reason we have been brought into existence at this time, in this place, with these people, that have been providentially placed in our lives, and we in theirs.

I will divert your attention for a couple of minutes to underscore the importance that you understand and accept what you just finished reading. Look again at that last line above. For if you have ever entertained the alluring fantasy of getting away from it all to live on some pristine body of water in a picturesque cabin totally isolated from the constant barrage of the cruel realities of our daily lives that are endlessly thrown at us in this world that seems to have gone completely mad, then you know by personal experience the truth of this topic. We may have not known it, but that fantasy just may be a desperate call for help and may be an unconscious admission that we do not yet have enough love readiness to face and fend off the awfulness of our world, and we may be yielding to the temptation to want to run and hide. If true, it is a regrettable admission of our own vulnerability. Our problem is not where we live but perhaps our lack of love readiness to cope with real life issues in the here and now. And just as Jesus had to make a hard decision to come to our sin-sick planet, that same decision faces us. That is why the rest of this chapter may be of extreme importance for you. Please accept my earnest invitation to optimistically read on. Jesus knows

Understanding God's Way of Managing the People in Your Life

exactly how you feel right now about all of this. Please pray and allow him to bring loving clarity to your mind.

Well before he needed it, Christ solidified his love readiness way back in the Garden of Eden. So clearly, we need to solidify our love readiness *before* we need to love our way through a tough or challenging situation. This is where we as Christians depart from the world's approach to addressing challenging times and difficult situations in life. This is not a casual difference, but a black and white difference. In fact, for you not to understand this, you may be seduced into trying one of the world's much glamorized approaches propagated by a celebrity in another shallow motivational speech. And if you do buy into the world's approach to living, it may put you on the road to hell with people cheering you on. You may even feel like you are making progress, and whatever progress you seemly are making will ensure your ultimate disastrous ending. I know these are some significant and strong statements. But before you give in to the temptation to water them down so they will appear more palatable and acceptable to you, hear me out. This is exactly where many well-meaning and sincere would-be Christians get it wrong and wonder why Christianity isn't working for them. Don't just read this next section, study it.

Let's begin with a Scripture which you may have never studied or even heard of; it contains a shocking truth that you may not want to hear. And before you start scratching your head, think this through with me.

> *Even if you go and fight courageously in battle, God will overthrow you before the enemy, for God has the power to help or to overthrow.*
> (2 Chr 25:8, NIV)

When we are going through some really tough terrain, often our well-intentioned friends who earnestly want to support us will say things to build up our confidence and encourage us forward courageously, just like the verse above says. In the neck of the woods where I grew up, I was told things like: buck up, put your big boy pants on, you can do it, try harder, give it all you've got, suck it up, when the going gets tough, the tough get going, believe in yourself. And if that is not enough, there are a hundred self-help books waiting for you on Amazon®. And to be very clear, this book is not one of them, I did not want to write a self-help book. This is not a try harder book. I wanted to do only one thing: provide you a roadmap for becoming totally satisfied with God every moment of every day!

I'm sure you've heard your share of these kinds of motivational expressions. We've all heard these, and we all probably have said some of these

Part B: Journey Joy Maker Six

kinds of things ourselves. But I want to share with you that there are times when these are exactly opposite of what God wants us to say or hear. He may not want you to try harder, but to be loved more!

Look again at the verse above and notice that even when we are fighting a difficult challenge with all the courage we can muster up; God will allow or even cause us to be defeated by the situation in which we are entangled. Slogging our way through a bitter and humbling situation by our own courageous strength is not always what God wants. And God does not want you to just grin and bear it. If we ever think that we won and declare a false victory because we fought a valiant fight, and perhaps destroyed an opponent based on our own strength, we may be taking yet another step away from God. We may become even more independent and more prideful. And we may even start glorying in our own self-sufficiency. And by contrast, he wants to teach us to depend on his power which is available to us as his children. In the midst of our failures and weaknesses is when we get God's life-changing messages. Like he said to Paul, "*My grace is sufficient for you.*" (See 2 Cor 12:9.) Personally, I've never been more loved than when I'm totally broken, and my self-pride reprimanded.

Specifically, in this chapter I'm asking you to narrow your focus from God's magnificent world-creating power, as wonderful as that is, and I would like for you to focus on God's prioritized power, his foundational love that is so wonderfully made available to each of us. The power of love is severely underrated and undervalued. This is the love needed to have love readiness instantly available when you encounter an injustice that would normally kindle your anger and cause you to harbor self-pity, and leaving you wanting and thinking as to how you can take some kind of revenge to make things right. This chapter provides you the kind of love readiness displayed by Christ when vileness was cast upon him during the crucifixion and he did not cast vileness in return. Why? Because he had love readiness. He had enough love to save the suffering thief on the cross next to him, and enough love to show compassion to the very soldiers now killing and mocking him, while at the same time showing love and care for his sobbing mother. All of this happened while he was painfully dying a torturous death with us in mind. That is the best picture in existence as to the power of having love readiness and what it can do for you and for the people around you who may be actively abusing you.

I have found it helpful to think of it this way: God has created in each of us a love tank. This is the place where our love readiness is stored. And when our love tank is empty, we are simply out of gas (out of love). This makes it impossible to live and respond proactively and lovingly to all the fiery darts aimed at us by Satan and his minions. (See Eph. 6:10.) An empty love tank makes us exceedingly vulnerable to hurt feelings, self-depreciation, bitterness, resentfulness, and on and on. Our joy suffers a dreadful death to these ugly feelings. We live in a world of people with sharp elbows, broken people who feel the need to blow out your candle just to let theirs shine. Rarely, if ever, will a day go by in which you will not feel rejection, diminishment, being wronged, devalued, overlooked, and other sad experiences and encounters. And if these occurrences do not come from people on the outside, your own mind can and will barrage you with unfriendly assaults and self-accusations. To respond to each of these harsh realities while being able to maintain your joyfulness, necessitates a full love tank filled to the brim with love readiness. The saddest and most defenseless people in the world are people prodding though their days with empty love tanks. They are the most susceptible to depression and negativity, Is that ever you? Not only can they not be used by God to love a hurting world, they cannot even feel enough love to deal with their own self-doubts. And to add insult to injury, because of the emptiness of their own love tank, they endlessly must hear and contend with their own heart's cries and pleading sobs for love. But so often, they don't know that it is the healing love that only Christ can and wants to give them that can take away all that joy-interrupting noise. So, in the absence of God's love, they begin doing desperate things. Like the old song says, they look for love in all the wrong places. This only guarantees that their worst days are yet ahead of them. They will now be sucked into an endless succession of bad decisions, sinking themselves deeper and deeper into despair. This must be one of the worst conditions known to man. God help all of us with this!

Okay, enough of these doom and gloom realities. How do we get and keep our love tanks full of love readiness that will prevent all that emotional sewage identified above? Well, you may be surprised to learn that it all begins in the morning! No, really, there is a distinct and observable pattern in the Bible that is essential, but easily missed or overlooked. Let me show it to you. The psalmist saw it, knew it and embraced it.

> *Let the morning bring me word of your unfailing love.* (Ps 143:8a, NIV)

Part B: Journey Joy Maker Six

He knew that we need to fill up our love tanks in the morning with a large dose of *unfailing love* before we start our day. Don't ever start your day with an empty love tank just because you are in a hurry to get started! Job number one every day is to look up and look for, pray for, be ready for, and wait for the coming of God's *unfailing love*. God is promising you that he will love you in the morning! And when his love arrives read what happens next. *Satisfy us in the morning with your unfailing love, that we may sing for joy . . .* (Ps 90:14a, NIV) This is the holy moment of the morning, where your attitude for the day is being formed and when it is born, you will *sing for joy*. Own and embrace this holy moment when your day's mindset is being created by his love. Read and reread this truth. This is foundational for having a good day. Note that word *satisfy*. God does not want you to start your day until you are satisfied, or when your love tank is full of love readiness! If you are not pleased to be alive and excited about living the day ahead with your life partner, Jesus, you have yet to be satisfied. Don't walk out the door without being fully armed with his unfailing love. Said simply, this means you have yet to allow God to fill your love tank with his unfailing love.

Study the depth of the truths of this next Scripture. *But I will sing of your strength, in the morning I will sing of your love; for you are my fortress, my refuge in times of trouble.* (Ps 59:16, NIV). Immediately notice the connection between your strength and God's love. Our strength does not come from our own willpower, it does not come from a well-meaning commitment to try harder in this new day. Did you get that? Self-talks don't work. Our real strength only comes from being loved (having a love tank full of love readiness), which is your only reliable source of strength. Then note that once you experience and drink in the powerful sweetness of his love in the morning of a new day, it says we are now ready for times of trouble. Is it all coming together in your mind? Once we are satisfied and our personal love tank is full of love, the verse says we are now ready with the strength for the day's challenges. We can now say to the day, "Bring it on, I'm ready!" Caution, you are not ready for tomorrow's challenges, that will not happen until tomorrow morning's unfailing love comes your way. But you can be assured that tomorrow morning, God will refill your love tank with just enough love to get you through tomorrow.

And just when you think it can't get any better, it does in this next morning Scripture. *Because of the LORD's great love, we are not consumed, for his compassions never fail. They are new every morning; great is your faithfulness.* (Lam 3:22–23, NIV) There is one last thing God needs to do for all of this to work in your personal behalf. You may have had a bad day yesterday, or maybe a whole string of bad days. God's morning routine wants this really to be a new day for you. And that cannot happen if you are still feeling guilty or defeated from things that happened in the days gone by. So, you will notice his morning plan invites and ensures that you can have a fresh start. Only God would put together a plan that does something like this. He is truly amazing! And notice in this verse that it makes it very clear that he is faithful to daily apply his compassion to all the wrongs of yesterday so you can get 100 percent free from all that heavy baggage that weighs you down. If you accept that, you will feel the freedom of being released from all the ugliness of days gone by. And more importantly, love readiness will start gushing into and filling your love tank. To top it all off, that verse makes it clear that this can happen to and for you, every morning. Really, have you ever heard anything so wonderful? As the song says he has no rival; he has no equal.

If you had any doubts about the importance of this morning routine of making sure your love tank is full of love readiness before you start your day, allow me to share one final scripture that will clinch it for you.

> *Very early in the morning, while it was still dark, Jesus got up, left the house and went off to a solitary place, where he prayed.* (Mark1:35, NIV)

The Bible makes it clear that Jesus practiced this same type of morning routine we've been discussing. And it is good for us to remember that without his morning talks with God, he would never have had enough love readiness to face, endure, and become victorious over the crucifixion. Thank God he kept his love tank full, or you and I would not have the blessed hope that keeps us going. I often wonder if this is why in the book of Revelation the Bible calls him the bright Morning Star. He certainly knew the power of morning's holy moments. Do we? Enjoy the words from the chorus of the old hymn, "Great is Thy Faithfulness".

> *Great is Thy faithfulness! Great is Thy faithfulness! Morning by morning new mercies I see; All I have needed Thy hand hath provided Great is Thy faithfulness, Lord, unto me!*

Part B: Journey Joy Maker Six

My Morning Moments

It's early in the morning when I first begin to wake,
my mind races to uncover what outcomes for the day are at stake,
what changes and corrections need to be examined,
and what new decisions I need to make.

It's easy in just a few moments of reflection
to become smothered by anxieties of worry.
My head's not even off the pillow yet, with so much to do, I'm already in a hurry.

My self-confidence is tired and weak, I'm already thinking of what could go bad.
But I'm reminded of God's divine interventions and because of him,
all the rescues I've had.

Once again, I feel his presence and his protective promises of this new day,
and once again I'm reminded of his investment in me,
so I believe every word he has to say.

His promises of unfailing love and his gifts of hope, peace, and rest,
are that for which my heart is hungry, and they ready me to past today's test.

When my morning prayers are done and I'm ready to go on my way,
my mind is full of hope as I hear his words echoing throughout the day.
You are my child, the sparkle in my eye, all the words I love to hear him say.

And when the sun goes down, and once again my pillow receives my head,
it's been a day of answered prayers, as I fall to sleep after my thank you has been said.

Good night Father-God, I will now sleep sound,
knowing in the morning, more new mercies will be found.

Understanding God's Way of Managing the People in Your Life

My Journal for My Journey

Who are the people in your life that you need to forgive in advance?

Describe how you intend to keep your love tank full.

Describe your morning routine that works for you.

I have given God permission to bring needy and irritating people into my life for me to love in His behalf—Yes__, No__.

7

Extracting Anxiety from Your Life

WE LIVE IN A heavily medicated world where anxiety disorders are running rampant. The two parts in this chapter hit these issues head on. In the entire Bible. I do not know of another area in the daily drama of living that is dealt with more decisively as anxiety. Part A has the potential of removing over 50 percent of your worry. Part B will show you how to eliminate the remaining 50 percent. Together, they deliver a strong one-two punch to knock worry and anxiety out of your life. I've prayed for your freedom from all the tension that could be in your life.

LaVon

Part A

Journey Joy Killer Seven

Worry Defeated

How to Live a Fearless Life

SEE EXACTLY WHAT GOD is promising you! Let him speak for himself. (No one, but no one, could say it better than God did in his Word, the Bible. Unhurriedly read it, let the words find their intended home in your own heart. May it fill every nook and cranny of your mind, heart, and soul with his peace made in heaven and painfully brought down to earth for you by our beloved Lord Jesus. Everything that God has ever done throughout the ages was done so he could give and support these promises to you. Feel his love and breathe in his peace as you slowly drink in each of his words. He died so he could give this set of promises to you so that you can have absolute faith in them. He has demonstrated that he is dead serious about them. He wants to be your sovereign God and care for you. He is so eager for you to hear this message of divine love and protection! Truer truth, you will never read.

> *And we know that God causes everything to work together for the good of those who love God and are called according to his purpose for them. (Rom 8:28, NLT)*

> *Don't worry about anything; instead, pray about everything. Tell God what you need and thank him for all he has done. Then you will experience God's peace, which exceeds anything we can understand. His peace will guard your hearts and minds as you live in Christ Jesus. (Phil 4:6, NLT)*

Part A: Journey Joy Killer Seven

That is why I tell you not to worry about everyday life—whether you have enough food and drink, or enough clothes to wear. Isn't life more than food, and your body more than clothing? Look at the birds. They don't plant or harvest or store food in barns, for your heavenly Father feeds them. And aren't you far more valuable to him than they are? Can all your worries add a single moment to your life? And why worry about your clothing? Look at the lilies of the field and how they grow. They don't work or make their clothing, yet Solomon in all his glory was not dressed as beautifully as they are. And if God cares so wonderfully for wildflowers that are here today and thrown into the fire tomorrow, he will certainly care for you. Why do you have so little faith? So, don't worry about these things, saying, "What will we eat? What will we drink? What will we wear?" These things dominate the thoughts of unbelievers, but your heavenly Father already knows all your needs. Seek the Kingdom of God above all else, and live righteously, and he will give you everything you need." (Matt 6:25-33, NLT)

So don't worry about tomorrow, for tomorrow will bring its own worries. Today's trouble is enough for today. (Matt 6:34, NLT)

Peace I leave with you; my peace I give you. I do not give to you as the world gives. Do not let your hearts be troubled and do not be afraid. (John 14:27, NIV)

Then you will experience God's peace, which exceeds anything we can understand. His peace will guard your hearts and minds as you live in Christ Jesus. (Phil 4:7, NLT)

But now, O Jacob, listen to the LORD who created you. O Israel, the one who formed you says, "Do not be afraid, for I have ransomed you. I have called you by name; you are mine. When you go through deep waters, I will be with you. When you go through rivers of difficulty, you will not drown. When you walk through the fire of oppression, you will not be burned up; the flames will not consume you." (Isa 43:1-2, NLT)

Give your burdens to the LORD, and he will take care of you. He will not permit the godly to slip and fall. (Ps 55:22, NLT)

Trust in the LORD with all your heart; do not depend on your own understanding. Seek his will in all you do, and he will show you which path to take. (Prov 3:5-6, NLT)

Extracting Anxiety from Your Life

> *So be strong and courageous! Do not be afraid and do not panic before them. For the LORD your God will personally go ahead of you. He will neither fail you nor abandon you.* (Deut 31:6, NLT)

Signed and sealed by God the Father, God the Son, and God the Holy Spirit.

Not only does God want you to hear and know these promises, he also wants to help you in believing and applying them to your life every minute of every day as you walk through the valley of the shadow of death. He wants you to have a passion for living fearlessly. He wants you to awake every morning with an unbridled enthusiasm in getting to live yet another day with him as your personal heavenly Father. He wants you to greet the dawn and to see his hand extended to you and show his happiness to live this day by your side. He wants you to know how much he loves taking care of you and looking over you. He loves making you smile. He wants you to be excited about where you are in your spiritual journey traveling through this world, and extremely excited about where you will end up with him in your forever home. There can be no doubt about it, this is the joyful and peace-packed way he intends for us to live! Any way of living that is filled with torment, anxiety, and fearfulness is 100 percent contrary to his design. Let's get started and allow God to make your life what he wants it to be, filled with peace and hope!

Let's begin our defeating worry where the Bible does. You cannot end up where you want to be unless you are willing to start where God wants you to be. Here is the first recorded occurrence of worry, anxiety, and fear. Read it, and as you do, underscore the evidence of these three negative and destructive emotional conditions. It comprises the very first picture of what these three sinful consequences do to us humans, and it's not pretty. It occurs immediately after and as a result of mankind's first sin when Adam and Eve ate from the forbidden tree in the Garden of Eden. Let's pick it up from there:

> *And they heard the sound of the LORD God walking in the garden in the cool of the day, and the man and his wife hid themselves from the presence of the LORD God among the trees of the garden. But the LORD God called to the man and said to him, "Where are you?" And he said, "I heard the sound of you in the garden, and I was afraid, because I was naked, and I hid myself." He said, "Who told you that you were naked? Have you eaten of the tree of which I commanded you not to eat?" The man said, "The woman whom you gave to be with me, she gave me fruit of the tree, and I ate." Then the LORD God*

Part A: Journey Joy Killer Seven

said to the woman, "What is this that you have done?" The woman said, "The serpent deceived me, and I ate." (Gen 3:8–13, (ESV)

Do you get and feel the tragic gravity of this situation? Until now, in this paradise of the garden, Adam and Eve enjoyed their sweet, innocent, and transparent relationship with each other and with God, the creator of the universe. Then shockingly, the peaceful tranquility was shattered, and history and creation were forever altered, spoiled, and ruined. This was all brought about by humans' rejection and rebellion of God's plan for their lives when God told them not to eat from the tree of the knowledge of good and evil. (See Gen. 2:17.)

They did what they shouldn't have and ate of the forbidden tree! Then we find Adam and Eve running and hiding from their God who created them, missing the unique specialness of walking in the garden in the cool of the day with their God. Instead, they cowered, trembling with fear, and hiding from God behind the garden's trees and bushes in shame. What a catastrophic change of events! This episode demonstrates and depicts the most accurate picture of a person consumed and condemned in their own worry, anxiety, and fear—cowering and trembling while hiding in shame and guilt from their God who loved them and has come to be with them in the cool of the day. Any minute without God is an unnecessary tragedy of tragedies.

One moment, they were breathing the pure air of freedom, 100 percent worry free and enjoying an atmosphere of a peaceful, contented life in paradise. Then their paradise ended abruptly by the disgrace of sin. Pause for a second and describe a world without worry, anxiety, and fear. However you would define it, that is a depiction and portrayal of what it was like living in the Garden of Eden, pre sin. It is also a foretaste of glory divine in eternity. And notice the contrasting awfulness of the fearfulness and panic attack anxieties of what we are experiencing in today's brutal and unforgiving world This is exactly what motivated Jesus to leave heaven's paradise to come and begin the rescuing and restoring process on an individual-by-individual basis to displace our worry, anxiety, and fear from our lives. Thank God that he is a God that sees and cares about the cruelty of worry and was and is willing to do something about it! Worry, by far, is the biggest, most aggressive, and relentless bully known to man. It continually beats you down until your desire to live fearlessly and adventurously has been crushed.

Extracting Anxiety from Your Life

But for God to defeat worry in our lives in this, our real and cursed world, we must acknowledge that there is an irrevocable tie between sin and worry that cannot and must not be denied. So, if we are going to claim victory over worry, anxiety, and fear we must begin where it began, with sin. All the disseminated worry solutions, and there are many, that do not deal with this foundational cause cannot and will not bring about a permanent or satisfying solution to calm the worried, quiet the anxious, and silence their fears. Pills will not do it, drinking will not do it, drugs will not do it, counseling will not do it, pep talks will not do it, mental trickery will not do it, and medication will not do it. We must talk about what very few people want to talk about—foundational sins. There is no help available that works until we deal with hidden sin. If you are resisting that thought right now, this may be a hard message for you to hear.

Take careful note of this: As Adam and Eve were trembling and hiding from God behind those trees and bushes in the garden, it was because they had guilty consciences. You see, worry, anxiety, and fear need fertile ground for them to grow and flourish in our minds. And that fertile ground is a guilty conscience. Once that is seen, all the Scriptures on this subject begin to make a lot of sense. Here is only a small but very powerful sampling.

> *So, I always take pains to have a clear conscience toward both God and man.* (Acts 24:16, ESV)
>
> *Therefore, one must be in subjection, not only to avoid God's wrath but also for the sake of conscience.* (Rom 13:5, ESV)
>
> *The aim of our charge is love that issues from a pure heart and a good conscience and a sincere faith.* (1 Tim 1:5, ESV)
>
> *Holding faith and a good conscience. By rejecting this, some have made shipwreck of their faith.* (1Tim 1:19, ESV)
>
> *They must hold the mystery of the faith with a clear conscience.* (1Tim 3:9, ESV)
>
> *Let us draw near with a true heart in full assurance of faith, with our hearts sprinkled clean from an evil conscience and our bodies washed with pure water.* (Heb 10:22, ESV)

This is exactly why this chapter is under the heading of journey joy killer. It is precisely the existence of these unacknowledged, besetting sins that can derail you and cause you to lose your joyfulness in living. A guilty conscience is an open invitation to worry, anxiety, and fear. The writer of Hebrews says it this way:

> *Therefore, since we are surrounded by so great a cloud of witnesses [who by faith have testified to the truth of God's absolute faithfulness], stripping off every unnecessary weight and the sin which so easily and cleverly entangles us, let us run with endurance and active persistence the race that is set before us.* (Heb 12:1, AMP)

The inescapable conclusion of all these Scriptures is that if we do not have a clear conscience, we are vulnerable to the destructive forces of worry, anxiety, and fear, just as was the case with Adam and Eve in the Garden of Eden. When we carry around an unrepented, unconfessed, undisclosed, and unforgiven sin, we cannot and will not be able to ever defeat worry. These emotions come from the same heart in which your hidden sin resides. And when sin exists in your heart, Satan can and will take that sinful crud and keep slamming it up against the walls of your mind's thoughts, and your confidence in yourself and in your future will shrink and dwindle until it is destroyed, allowing worry, anxiety, and fear to sprout and flourish and take its place. You won't hate sin until you understand and hate what sin does and is doing to you! Sin will derail you, period! Although not the only cause, sin is the primary cause of worry, anxiety, and fear.

If you are serious about defeating worry in your life you must take first things first, you must come clean. Find a Christian buddy, or a caring pastor, repent and confess the presence of hidden sin, and accept God's grace to receive absolute and total forgiveness. Make yourself accountable to a Christian buddy who loves you enough to hold you accountable until that sin is completely eradicated from your life. Once your conscience is clear, you have established or confirmed that the foundation is in place for you to be able to defeat worry.

In case you are wondering, yes, you can experience worry even when there is no specific sin to which it can directly be linked. But even in those cases, it is always a good idea to make sure you are not harboring some hidden sin which has not been eradicated from your life, and for which you have not received forgiveness. With a clear conscience as your foundation, you can then live a worry-free life by taking the following precautions listed below.

Did you know that being worried is a matter of choice? Yeah, you heard that right, you can decide not to worry. Please allow me to explain. Here are the two choices for which you must accept responsibility if you

Extracting Anxiety from Your Life

want to defeat the malignant, emotional cancer of worry which can and will take over and ruin your life. Remember, worry is a journey joy killer!

Decision and Choice 1: Decide the timeframe and put boundaries around the time period in which you will allow worry. This is not a suggestion, it is a command of Christ who said, *"Therefore do not be anxious about tomorrow, for tomorrow will be anxious for itself. Sufficient for the day is its own trouble."* (Matt 6:34, ESV) God has promised that he will provide you all the grace needed to handle today's problems and challenges. Tomorrow's grace will not be available until then. God wants us to focus on what is on our plate right now, today. If you are focused on the future, you will miss living out the will of God today. You must not sacrifice today for tomorrow's troubles. When worries that pertain to future possible problems crop up in your mind, you must decide to call them out by speaking to them and saying, "I am putting you in God's capable hands until it's time for me to become involved. Until then, I'm going to focus all my energies on accomplishing what God wants me to accomplish today."

By making just this one decision, you will have removed most of the worry from your life.

Decision and Choice 2: Decide when you will walk by faith as opposed to walking by sight. Every time you feel a tinge of worry beginning to erupt, you have a decision to make. Will you address this worry by sight or by faith? This is what is at stake:

> *And without faith it is impossible to please him, for whoever would draw near to God must believe that he exists and that he rewards those who seek him."* (Heb 11:6, ESV)

This makes it clear that if you, by default, allow a challenging issue to spark worry in your life because of a disturbing tendency to walk by sight, as opposed to putting this challenge into the faith category, you will be forfeiting God's personal involvement plus his reward for having trusted him. This is a loss you cannot afford if you want to live a joyful and productive life. To do nothing and allow worry to raise its ugly head is to, by default, to be walking by sight. You must decide to walk by faith! Again, to walk by faith means that you consciously decide to turn things over to God.

I opened this chapter by grouping a bunch of my favorite scriptural promises together. Immediately, when that little tinge of worry first hits you, speak one or more of those promises (or one of your own favorites) directly to the worry. Then turn to God and thank God for that promise as you quote it to him. That is how you defeat new worries that pop up on

Part A: Journey Joy Killer Seven

a regular basis. Do not let them have a home in your thinking. Never play host to a worry, quickly speak scriptural truth to them! They will wilt away as you magnify God's personal involvement in your life and invite him to partner with you in all your challenges. Run to Daddy! He is lovingly waiting! That is why he is called our heavenly Father. Live worry free!

Extracting Anxiety from Your Life

What Have I to Worry?

With the news daily broadcasting all the world's dastardly deeds,
because journalists subscribe to the proven principle, if it bleeds, it reads.

So we get our daily dose of mankind's most heinous sins,
showcasing the evilest among us as the one who usually wins.

We are in a world that has gone horribly wrong,
A world upside down in which we weren't intended to belong.

It seems that every day we are hit with some new bad news.
There's always a new problem waiting that leaves me confused.

What should I do? Should I run or just shiver in fear?
Do I hold tight to the people and things I hold dear?

But from heaven's vantage point Jesus both saw and felt my worry's harm,
a malignant blight on our souls, his creation now in crises sounded an alarm.

Leaving his heaven, the place for which my heart does crave,
he came to rescue me by going to the grave.

He fought the fight that I could not fight,
and by paying its price, he made justice right.

Now with confidence, I can approach the throne of grace,
Gone is my fear of living and dying in disgrace.

The comfort of his presence with the power of his resurrection,
Have defeated the cruelty of anxiety and the fear from worry's infection.

Part A: Journey Joy Killer Seven

His amazing gift of allowing and enabling me to live a life free from worry,
by taking the weight of my fears and anxieties, on the cross that he did carry.

Because of that, never again a day without him will I ever spend.
He's my Savior, my Lord. and now also, my best friend.

He's given me a way to live worry free,
both now and for all eternity!

Extracting Anxiety from Your Life

My Journal for My Journey

The recurring things about which I often worry about are . . .

As a result of reading this chapter, I plan to . . .

Here is how I plan on containing my attention to today, allowing God to handle tomorrow . . .

I Confess I habitually worry about the following issues . . .

Part B

Journey Joy Maker Seven

Living Behind God's Line of Protection

How to Be and Live Victim Free!

For those of us in relationship with Christ, we have been given a coveted promise to which we can cling in our desperate and challenging hours. Available to us is God's safe space. It gives us both an emotional sanity and security, even in the very worst of times. It, and it alone, enables us to escape the confining prison of victimhood, knowing that an ultimate and unassailable wall of protection separates me from ever needing to be or feel or think like a victim. In fact, if I feel like a victim, that is a sure sign that I've stopped believing in and accepting that wonderful and providential promised line of protection that surrounds our safe space, and I have foolishly abandoned the precious value of being in relationship with Jesus Christ and all the wonderful benefits it entails. These are the privileged gains that cannot be obtained from anywhere, anyway, anyhow, and from anyone else, only from and through Jesus!

Here is his written guarantee to us: This is one of eighteen specific promises identified in my book entitled *Untangling the Seven Desires of your Heart*.

> *No temptation has overtaken you that is not common to man. God is faithful, and he will not let you be tempted beyond your ability, but with the temptation he will also provide the way of escape, that you may be able to endure it.* (1 Cor 10:13, ESV)

Extracting Anxiety from Your Life

Our Vulnerability

Do we know our own ability or inability to handle things? Do we know our own limitations? Or do we allow our fears and anxieties to take over as we plunge into that deep pit of emotional victimhood? Does my world ever turn to an unwelcoming and scary darkness? Am I sacrificing the very reason I believe, and have I begun to doubt the whole reason I've reached out to God in the first place? Do I not understand the very motive of why God exists and why he lovingly brought me into existence? Have I become confused about his purpose for me and for my being alive? Have I forgotten the price he had to pay for me that makes me of great worth to him? Has my destiny now become unclear? Do I no longer understand that God is always focused on little old me and that his mighty power is behind the rustle of every leaf. Has my weakened faith suffered a devastating blow of doubt? Has Satan succeeded in reducing me to a small, fragile, sniveling, and whimpering pile of worthless victimhood? Am I wallowing in a miserable pool of self-pity? Have I allowed myself to become a defenseless, abandoned piece of humanity, rotting away with time, waiting to be thrown into the dung heap of history?

If you take the above biblical promise away from your everyday consciousness, then the words in the former paragraph and their descriptions will become real and dominate your thinking and feelings, all of which have been brought on by allowing yourselves to become a victim. For those of us who tend to be cocky and proud and pride ourselves in our own self-sufficiency, we will respond to our victim feelings by lashing out at our supposed victim-makers with a self-righteous vengeance of entitlement, demanding our due and making them pay a price. For those of us who are humbler and are often filled with self-doubts or second-guess ourselves, we will be tempted to shrivel up to nothingness and obscurity while cowering in the shadows.

Those two extremes are contrary to God's will for our lives, and both are nothing more or nothing less than Satan's fantasies and delusions that he delivers to our minds once we open our door to him by seeing ourselves as victims. And when we head into either one of these two reactive directions (self-proud or self-defeated), we become willing slaves to Satan's whims, and we will be used by him to hurt and/or destroy others or to hurt or destroy our own selves. And when that happens, a valuable and non-replaceable piece of God's creation will have been needlessly destroyed, a calamity of all calamities! Satan will have succeeded in marginalizing our greatness and will have diminished our usability by God. We will have allowed Satan to attain his ultimate goal by using our demise to hurt and inflict pain on God, who grieves over our every pain and suffering. Satan knows full well that he can inflict hurt on God by hurting us. This is true because we are God's valued treasures, we are precious in his sight, and we are treasured in his heart! And that is the precise reason there is a line of protection surrounding each of us! Any moment that we stop believing in that line of protection by allowing ourselves to become victims, we make ourselves instantly vulnerable.

Our Choice

Where we do not have a choice is, Will we be victimized? Of course, we have all been made a
victim and we will be made a victim again and again. And it is not just because we live in an unfair world, which we do. It is because Satan's playbook always begins with making us feel like a victim. He is brilliant at making us feel mistreated and offended. Beginning in Genesis 3 with Adam and Eve and all the way to you and I, he continuously orchestrates us into feeling robbed, duped, and unfairly wronged. He uses anything from nations, governments, family, colleagues, neighbors, friends, strangers, and even our own selves—often, we are our own harshest critics—to harm and insult us. Once he has us feeling cheated, he can quickly move us into the selfish feelings of entitlement, where we boldly begin taking life into our own hands. And inch by inch we unknowingly move forward to becoming our own god, casting off his moral restraints one at a time, to do what we think we need to do. In short, we will have just chosen the wrong fork in the road and now we are mindlessly headed into Satan's hell. We have devolved into becoming Satan's pawns on his world chessboard, his battlefield where ruined lives are made and callously discarded.

So herein lies our choice: We can be victimized, but we can also choose not to become a victim. By grace, our lives have been redefined by getting into a relationship with Christ. Things no longer happen to us: they happen for us! The same watchful eye of God that is on the sparrow is also on us. But we must be willing to relax in his hands knowing that the sovereign God of the universe is completely in control, and as his children, He cares for us and surrounds us with a line of protection. And because of this line,

Extracting Anxiety from Your Life

we each can know: He (God) knows our limits and will not allow anything to happen to us that would exceed our limitations.

- Whatever happens God will use it for me, and I will emerge closer to him and better prepared to achieve the purpose he has for me.
- I don't need to know what's ahead because I know that he knows and has drawn a line of protection around me.
- I can embrace and rest in his unfailing love even in the worst of times.
- Because he is God, I don't need to be, and I don't need to take things into my own hands,
- That the outcome is not dependent on me, it is dependent on him, so I can take a deep breath of relief and be filled with a deep sense of gratitude.
- That I can now go from being a victim to becoming a victor!

Read it again:

> *No temptation has overtaken you that is not common to man. God is faithful, and he will not let you be tempted beyond your ability, but with the temptation he will also provide the way of escape, that you may be able to endure it.* (1 Cor 10:13, ESV) Thank God, there is a limit!

Part B: Journey Joy Maker Seven

I'm Victim Free

In a world known for its brutality that is grossly unfair and unjust,
I often sense the pain of being mistreated, consuming me with disgust.

Sometimes it fills me with anger, other times I'm just victimized and sad.
Either way, it is not the way that God wants me to live, feeling so bad.

We are all being sucked downward by this world's evil gravity,
its Satan's way to disrupt and destroy our heavenly destiny.

By Satan's design, I find myself embroiled with smoldering self-pity,
wishing instead that I was in eternity, living in the Holy City.

I try telling myself to be patient and willing to wait until heaven when all will be well,
but I don't think I can make it until then and living as a victim in this emotional hell.

But God knows me better and came from heaven to hand me a key,
a new door to open, through which I can go and be forever victim free.

He takes everything that happens to me and transforms it to be for me.
Giving it to him allows him to grow me into what I was meant to be.

It is almost too unreal to say that everything that happens he allows for my good.
I can now confront Satan's words of defeat and not be hindered by his favorite falsehood.

From victim to victor, God has enabled me to be,
from victim's prison, I now have been set free.

Regardless of what comes my way and what cards I'm dealt,
I can continue in God's joy with a freedom that is deeply felt.

Extracting Anxiety from Your Life

Because of him, I'm victim free,
now and for all eternity!

All because of what Jesus is doing for me,
enabling me now to live on planet earth joyfully.

Thanks be to God; I am living victim free.

Part B: Journey Joy Maker Seven

My Journal for My Journey

Describe a time when you were or are feeling like a victim . . .

The Scripture talks about God providing us a way of escape. Tell about a time when God gave you a way of escape . . .

Do you believe God limits what can happen to you? If so, how does that make you feel?

Knowing there is a "line of protection," it makes me feel . . .

8

Winning the Final Battle for Your Soul before It's Fought

WE NOW COME TO the last chapter in the book and I have so many more things I would like to discuss. I'm told that people today won't read long books like they used to. But I do want to discuss Satan's strategy as you get older and want you to be fully prepared for his final assault on you. So, this chapter is to make sure you are fully armed and ready to declare victory before the battle is fought. Part A will walk you out on that final battle ground, and Part B will provide you a road map for ending life being empowered. I think you will really enjoy these two segments dedicated to making sure you are living a victorious life.

As always, remember we are in his mighty love and his mighty grip,

LaVon

Part A

Journey Joy Killer Eight

Knowing and Defeating Satan's Strategy

The Final Battleground for Your Soul

HERE ARE QUESTIONS THAT you may not have asked yourself. Are you, at this very moment, living without a consciousness of the biblical certainly that you are going to die at any moment, anytime, anywhere, or are you putting it out of your mind? Do you currently have a distorted view of how to approach those final years and days of your life? If so, you are exactly where Satan has wanted you since the beginning of time. His first recorded lie was,

> *Then the serpent said to the woman, "You will not surely die."* (Gen 3:4, NKJV)

Satan knew that until Eve discounted and questioned death (saw death differently than God), he would not be able to seduce her in to eating the forbidden fruit. Death, deceit, and the devil constitute an evil trinity resulting in the deadly consequences of disobedience.

Satan is extremely active with death and uses it to accomplish his purposes. Notice how the Bible describes Satan's relationship with death.

> *We are people of flesh and blood. That is why Jesus became one of us. He died to destroy the devil, who had power over death. But he also died to rescue all of us who live each day in fear of dying.* (Heb 2:14–15, CEV)

To be clear, Satan weaponizes our deaths (your death and my death) to steer us in a direction that separates us from God into eternal death. He used the death lie in the Garden of Eden, and he is doing it now with you and me. So that begs the question, is he doing it to us at this very moment? If so, what does his death lie sound like today?

Once you understand these truths around the relationship between Satan and your death, you can begin to appreciate the seriousness of this subject. It is about the issues emanating from this deadly duel of the devil and death, which this book addresses. Our relentless journey as we march towards our personal bodily demise will eventually and always bring us into the final battle ground where Satan contests for our souls. This ending part of our life journey is in the crosshairs of Satan's attention. This is the most concentrated time in our lives where Satan is intensely focused on deceiving us. Regarding our eternal destiny, this is the proverbial do or die time of our earthy pilgrimage. This book has called out some of Satan's death lies and has provided some of the biblical cautions in navigating our own chosen personal journeys to our grave, thus fulfilling our destiny in a cursed world.

> *Just as people are destined to die once, and after that to face judgment.* (Heb 9:27, NIV)

As in the days of old, I pray this book has prepared you to willingly march out on that final battleground of old age with your head held high, knowing where you stand and in whom you believe.

> *The LORD your God, who is going before you, will fight for you.* (Deut 1:30a, NIV)

What happens at death and immediately after death was not the main purpose of this book. I assume that you already believe in the splendor of heaven where we will be pleasured to bask in the presence of our loving and personal Lord forever! This book is all about your personal approach to journeying through your life as you get older, your mindset for eventually growing old, eventually entering those final years before you die, the choices you will have to make concerning your priorities along the journey, your joyful lifestyle, and your mental state of mind gushing with hope as you reach those last days. The content of this book is to prepare you long before you go out on that final battlefield where you will meet Satan's last ferocious and vicious battle for your soul. And you will boldly say with Paul:

> *For I am now ready to be offered, and the time of my departure is at hand. I have fought a good fight, I have finished my course, I have kept the faith: Henceforth there is laid up for me a crown of righteousness, which the Lord, the righteous judge, shall give me at*

Part A: Journey Joy Killer Eight

that day: and not to me only, but unto all them also that love his appearing. (2 Tim, 4: 6–8, KJV)

If you are still concerned or uncomfortable about death, I invite you to think about and the personal significance of six verses (pictures of heaven). They constitute six different scriptural snapshots of God's view of what a perfect personal environment looks and feels like. It gives you a chance to have a sneak preview of what God has in mind for us in heaven. God, in his wisdom and love, wants all of us to be enchanted by heaven, so the Bible reveals to us these six different heavenly views as to what it will be like for us when we get there. We all go through different seasons in our lives, so depending on where you are right now as you read this, most likely one or two of these will immediately ring true in your heart more so than the others. As you read them, be conscious as to the comforting feelings it brings to you. Circle the one(s) that have the greatest emotional appeal to you and ask yourself why it is having this kind of impact on you at this time in your life.

1. For those of us who have not or currently are not experiencing the love and continued comforts of a satisfying home, heaven is a perfect place that will be home to us forever. *My Father's house has many rooms; if that were not so, would I have told you that I am going there to prepare a place for you? And if I go and prepare a place for you, I will come back and take you to be with me that you also may be where I am.* (John 14:2–3, NIV) The reason Jesus shares this with us is so we can dream and know with certainty that we have a heavenly home with our name on it.

2. Many of us have yearned of taking a dream vacation to see things that others have seen, but we have not, nor do we have the resources to even think we will be able to see them someday in the future. Our heart aches to see all the beautiful places that God has made. The Bible's view of heaven says that we will have an unequaled and thrilling adventure to see and witness the most wonderful things and places beyond our wildest imagination. *What no eye has seen, what no ear has heard, and what no human mind has conceived—the things God has prepared for those who love him.* (1 Cor 2:9, NIV)

3. Let this one sink in, it is how Isaiah described heaven. It is for those of us who are bothered about all the injustices and inequalities of this life. Heaven is a place where there is no more injustice. It is a place

where all wrongs will be made right. *They will build houses and dwell in them; they will plant vineyards and eat their fruit. No longer will they build houses and others live in them, or plant and others eat. For as the days of a tree, so will be the days of my people; My chosen ones will long enjoy the works of their hands. They will not labor in vain, nor will they bear children doomed to misfortune; for they will be a people blessed by the LORD, they and their descendants with them.* (Isa 65:21–23, NIV)

4. For those of us who are so tired of violence, and the fear of hurt and death, heaven's peace will pervade even the animal kingdom. *The wolf and the lamb will feed together, and the lion will eat straw like the ox, and dust will be the serpent's food. They will neither harm nor destroy in all my holy mountain., says the LORD.* (Isa 65:25, NIV)

5. For those of us who have had to contend with our own feebleness and physical limitations, heaven will a place where the weak and handicapped will be healed and made strong, no more physical constraints. *Then will the eyes of the blind be opened and the ears of the deaf unstopped. Then will the lame leap like a deer, and the mute tongue shout for joy. Water will gush forth in the wilderness and streams in the desert.* (Isa 35:5–6, NIV)

6. For those of us who have experienced unusual and long hardships and suffering, heaven will be a place where God will live with his people and there will be an end to loneliness, death, crying, and pain. *And I heard a loud voice from the throne saying, "Look! God's dwelling place is now among the people, and he will dwell with them. They will be his people, and God himself will be with them and be their God. 'He will wipe every tear from their eyes. There will be no more death or mourning or crying or pain, for the old order of things has passed away."* (Rev 21:3–4, NIV)

Believe in and live for heaven. There is no better place and no better way to think about your eternal destiny immediately beyond death! God shared these heavenly insights so that in our times of sadness, or loneliness, or discouragement, or doubt, we can be helped and encouraged by having the knowledge and hope of heaven, a kind of future homesickness for the place we will someday soon call home.

Part A: Journey Joy Killer Eight

I May Be Growing Older, but I'm Also Growing Bolder

All our life we fight growing old,
old age is the pits, or so we are told.
They say we will be mentally and physically limited.
Lies, all damn lies, spouted by the age bigoted.
They echo the words from Satan's lies on death.
Who wants us to tremble up until our final breath?

Should we weaken and succumb to his final battle cry,
he will have succeeded to hold us hostage right up until we die.

No, Satan, a thousand and one no's,
for we've been rescued by one who before us goes.

Yes, you had him drag that cross up Calvary's hill,
and yes, you got the Roman soldiers him to kill.

And yes, on that cruel cross he gave up his final breath.
And yes, the ignorant mob was quick to announce his brutal death.

But in God's exact timing in Earth's history,
when hope was in peril as Jesus was taken off that tree,
he was placed in a grave prepared for the dead,
the whole world was shocked when he arose instead.

And because of that, we say, "Oh death where is your sting?"
For us, it's time to let the celebration bells ring.
I will forever rejoice as the angels sing
For now, I'm forever home with my King!

Winning the Final Battle for Your Soul before It's Fought

> Dying and death have been defeated
> And Satan, your plans for me have now been cheated.

So when this corruptible shall have put on incorruption, and this mortal shall have put on immortality, then shall be brought to pass the saying that is written, Death is swallowed up in victory. O death, where is thy sting? O grave, where is thy victory? The sting of death is sin; and the strength of sin is the law. But thanks be to God, which giveth us the victory through our Lord Jesus Christ. (1 Cor 15:54–57, KJV)

Part A: Journey Joy Killer Eight

My Journal for My Journey

When I think about death, it makes me feel . . .

I am ready to get old because . . .

When I think about heaven, the best thing about going there and being there is . . .

My thoughts and feelings about my aging process are . . .

Part B
Journey Joy Maker Eight

Managing the Crossover Effect

We Are Either Empowered or Enfeebled by Our Journey

THERE IS A SET of decisions that all of us have the liberty and privilege to make. But many of us have not thought about them or have been apprised that these decisions even exist, let alone being forewarned as to the consequences of not making any decisions in this critical area. Making them can unleash the enormous potential that each of us possess to do good and that will eternally impact those that God, by his divine providence, wants to bring into our lives. He designed us with a purpose that was built into us in our mother's womb.

> *For we are his workmanship, created in Christ Jesus for good works, which God prepared beforehand, that we should walk in them.* (Eph 2:10, ESV)

Notice that last line, *that we should walk in them.* When that happens, and if that happens, is dependent on how well we manage the crossover effect. This verse makes it clear that there is a path for each of us on which God wants us to walk, but there are decisions that need to be made concerning allowing God to make that walk happen in our lives.

It denotes a time in our lives where we attain and allow the maturity of our spiritual knowledge and wisdom for godly living to overtake and eclipse, both in importance and power, our mental and physical ability to perform work; hence I call it the crossover effect. And when that happens, we will find ourselves on an upward trend called empowerment. By way of contrast, if the crossover effect is ignored and life-giving decisions are not made, we will find ourselves on a downward trend called enfeeblement, which will only intensify each and every day as we get older. That is why this is such a core concept, and if we are serious about journeying God's way, there are only two directions from which you can choose. Jesus, in very clear and strong language, says it this way:

> *"Enter by the narrow gate. For the gate is wide and the way is easy that leads to destruction, and those who enter by it are many. For the gate is narrow and the way is hard that leads to life, and those who find it are few."* (Matt 7:13–14, ESV)

Please allow me to hit the pause button and explain how and where I came up with this concept. I had a three-hour layover in Tokyo on my way back from Hong Kong. And while sitting in that busy airport, I was contemplating the Scripture above where Jesus said those who find this narrow way are few. As I observed the teeming mass of people surrounding me in this very large and congested airport, I tried to imagine the ratio of people who entered the narrow gate as opposed to the number of people entering the wide gate that leads to destruction. Is it one in five, one in ten, one in fifty, or one in a hundred? Would I answer it differently if I were in a different airport in another country, or in America? As I continued to ponder this question, I grew sadder and sadder and I felt the hurt in God's heart. Truly what Jesus said, *". . . Look at the fields, because they are ready for harvest"* (John 4:25, CSB) is truer today than ever before! That is when and where I decided that this concept needed to be captured in this book. The contrasting definitions of these two very different pathways that that are available to each of us can be stated this way:

- Empowerment: The precious Scripture (Matt 7:13–14) refers to this as life. Empowerment involves the ability to stay relevant to and for God by making applicable and wise contributions to those who God will continuously bring into our lives. God can and wants to be endlessly using us, right up to our point of death. If we are empowered, God is winning in our lives! He is optimizing the potential he designed in us at conception! We have a divine sense of worth from enabling God to use us to love others in a thousand different ways.

- Enfeeblement: In that same verse, the Bible refers to this as destruction. This is the ongoing, progressive deterioration of our mental and physical abilities to function and perform God's intended purpose in and through us at normal, healthy, and satisfying levels. If we are not being empowered by God's wisdom and his presence, coupled with the fact that we are progressively getting older and our health may be beginning to inhibit us, it becomes increasingly difficult for God to use us to serve our fellowman. Consequently, our self-esteem plunges along with our sense of worth. Satan is winning in our lives; he is quenching the very potential God designed in us at our conception.

You can tell if or when you are proactively managing the crossover effect when you begin deriving your sense of worth and importance from God using you to lead and inspire others to be closer to Jesus through the wisdom you've received by God's grace through and from your earthly years of pain and suffering. You have decided to grow in grace and knowledge (2 Pet 3:18) as opposed to getting your sense of importance from your intelligence, looks, beauty, strength, athleticism, or work accomplishments. These attributes and accomplishments are not evil or bad but need to be subjugated to the glory of Christ and the advancement of his kingdom. If that does not happen, they will have become a spiritual impediment to you. The Bible would now classify them as your idols that you are knowingly or unknowingly pursuing and serving. And as aging happens, and you lose these very things on which you were dependent for being relevant and of worth, you will be left empty or, if you please, enfeebled. Nothing is sadder than being around a once beautiful and attractive woman who became dependent on her good looks, but now age has extracted its fleshly price and her attractiveness has begun fading. And if she has failed to manage the decisions around the crossover effect, her self-esteem will be plummeting. The same is true of a superstar athlete when his aging extracts its pound of flesh and his athletic prowess is reduced to only a fading memory of yesteryear, and he begins spiraling down into a mere shadow of himself. He now feels diminished from his enfeeblement. These are only a of couple examples of failing to manage the decisions surrounding the crossover effect and as a result will experience the cruelty of aging.

Study the following model and begin thinking about where you are in self-managing the crossover effect.

Part B: Journey Joy Maker Eight

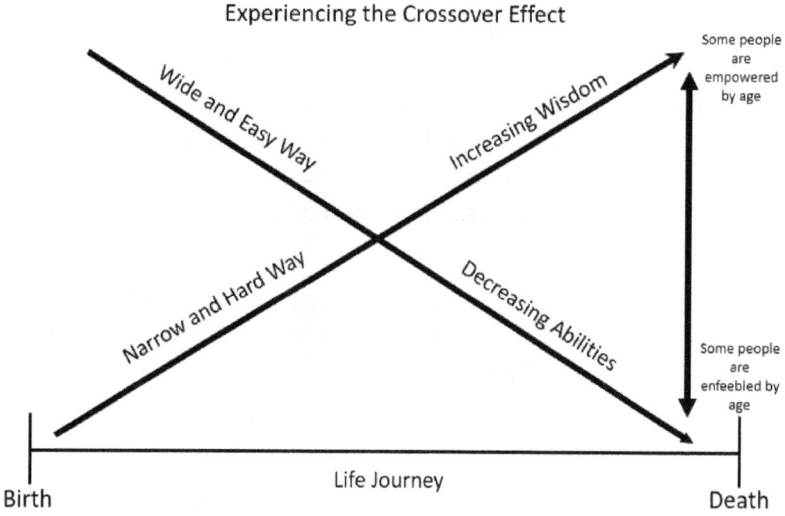

Since you are not yet dead yet and you are reading this book, then you still have options where you have the freedom to make proactive decisions. These options are demanding your attention and begging you for decisions to be made. (It should be noted that sometimes our ability and freedom to decide in any one of these areas may be taken away from us at any time due to events outside of our control, i.e., accidents, disasters, diseases, etc.) But for most of us, we can still make life-changing decisions that will dramatically affect the crossover effect on how we age and how we end our lives. In the previous chapters, we discussed numerous ways to ensure a higher quality end of life experience by proactively beginning to manage the crossover effect by removing joy killers and embracing joy makers. Doing so ensures that you will be empowered by your journey's aging progress.

Benjamin Franklin said, "Life's biggest tragedy is that we get old too soon and wise too late." Once people understand it, everyone wants to experience empowerment as early in life as is possible. But I would hasten to say, it is never too late to want to experience empowerment regardless of age. But to younger readers of this book, may I have the privilege of showing you the unbelievable and unmatchable benefits of experiencing an early crossover effect?

It means that you wisely and willingly have avoided the lure of entering life's journey through the wide and easy gate, and have followed the guidance of Jesus, and have begun a lifestyle that many would see as hard and difficult as opposed to a more popular and conveniently easy life journey. You have made a prudent decision and are now entering the narrow gate that leads to life, or empowerment, as it is referred to above.

First, you are to be congratulated; you have just joined the ranks of two of my biblical heroes: David, who killed Goliath the giant as a teenager and became the young warrior king of Israel, and Timothy, the young and wise leader in the early Christian community who was mentored by Paul who told him:

> *"This charge I entrust to you, Timothy, my child, in accordance with the prophecies previously made about you, that by them you may wage the good warfare"* (1 Tim 1:18, ESV)

> *Let no one despise you for your youth, but set the believers an example in speech, in conduct, in love, in faith, in purity.* (1 Tim 4:12, ESV)

Secondly, just because you have rightly chosen to prioritize the development of godly wisdom, it does not mean that you can or should devalue your reliance on your physical and mental health. The goal is not to prioritize it above your spiritual wisdom. Notice the careful wording of Paul on how he mentors young Timothy when he talks to him about his physical exercise program as it relates to his spiritual wisdom development.

> *. . . You will be a good servant of Christ Jesus, being trained in the words of the faith and of the good doctrine that you have followed. Have nothing to do with irreverent, silly, myths. Rather train yourself for godliness; for while bodily training is of some value, godliness is of value in every way, as it holds promise for the present life and also for the life to come.* (1 Tim 4: 6b–8, ESV)

Jesus is concerned about why we do what we do. We should exercise because of our responsibility to care for our bodies and minds, both of which are gifts of God requiring good stewardship. We do not physically exercise to vaunt up our pride in how good we look. We exercise because we do not have permission to mistreat any gift of God. And as we progress in years, and by necessity, we will need to be vigilant in our stewardship responsibilities for our physical and mental health and wellbeing.

Each of us has the freedom as to what form that will take, but ignoring our health is never an option. Whether you choose to go to the gym, or you choose to just park farther away and take the stairs, it is your choice. But honoring your stewardship responsibilities is a must. A well-maintained body does not detract from God being glorified by your looks, but a sloppy,

Part B: Journey Joy Maker Eight

out-of-shape and obese body may. There, I said it. You and God can prayerfully determine what needs to be done in your life right now. Take a deep breath and make any necessary decisions that may have been neglected for far too long. But know this, Jesus still loves you 100 percent, but he also wants to use you to your 100 percent potential. Get rid of anything that could be hindering that and your joy will be full!

Let's now turn our attention to developing godly wisdom, the true source of our empowerment. As we get older, we should be getting wiser. Here are some biblical insights for enabling that to happen. Check the boxes of the areas in which you feel you are growing in godly wisdom. It will confirm if you are on the right road in proactively managing the crossover effect.

Are you asking God how to lead and love the people in your life? Wisdom begins when we ask God to be the Lord of our thinking.

> *"So give your servant a discerning heart to govern your people and to distinguish between right and wrong. "* (1 Kings 3:9a, NIV)

The list is almost endless as to where we need God's wisdom with the people in our own worlds—parental wisdom, employee and work colleague wisdom, ministry wisdom, friendship wisdom, marriage wisdom, neighborly wisdom, and on and on and on.

- Are you receiving practical and everyday living wisdom from God's word?
- Life is filled with tough decisions and we daily face adversaries and challenges, all of which require wisdom beyond our abilities to discern what is the right response to what life is throwing at us. *Oh, how I love your law! I meditate on it all day long. Your commands are always with me and make me wiser than my enemies* (Ps 119:97–98, NIV) From where are you getting your confidence to face another day?
- Nothing is more revealing than identifying the source of your self-assurance to tackle yet another day of life. *The fear of the LORD is the beginning of knowledge, but fools despise wisdom and instruction.*(Prov 1:7, NIV) As you grow in your ability to trust in the Lord for his daily protection and direction, you are growing and gaining in wisdom.
- How do you interpret life situations in which you find yourself? Wisdom is the ability to see life from God's perspective and then to know the best course of action to take. *How wonderful to be wise, to*

understand things, to be able to analyze them and interpret them. Wisdom lights up a man's face, softening its hardness. (Eccl 8:1, TLB)

Our views are small and filled with preconditioned biases and tainted with our fears coming from our weaknesses. Without God's wisdom, life situations do not make eternal sense.

- As we travel forward on the wisdom road, we will be encouraged by the things people say that they see in our lives. If we are connected to the heart of Jesus, we will be like him and be wiser. The people in our world will notice the difference between us and the people in their world. We will have become a reflection of the life of Jesus. *And the child grew and became strong; he was filled with wisdom, and the grace of God was on him.* (Luke 2:40, NIV) Are you involving God in your daily decision-making?

Life is an endless river of options flooding over us every day. If we believe the Bible when it tells us our hearts are deceitful, we will not trust ourselves to make the hundreds of choices confronting us without seeking the counsel of God. *If you want to know what God wants you to do, ask him, and he will gladly tell you, for he is always ready to give a bountiful supply of wisdom to all who ask him; he will not resent it.* (James 1:5, TLB). This is one of the best invitations you will ever receive.

On what information are you building your life philosophy?

True wisdom does not come from men's philosophies and ideas. *Don't let others spoil your faith and joy with their philosophies, their wrong and shallow answers built on men's thoughts and ideas, instead of on what Christ has said.* (Col 2:8, TLB) Be wise as to how you arrive at the real meaning of life.

On this side of heaven, none of us score 100 percent in the boxes above. But if reading through that short wisdom list you can see yourself growing in those areas, you can be assured you are on the road to empowerment and as you get older, empowerment will be your comforting friend as your body experiences enfeeblement, your aging enemy.

Part B: Journey Joy Maker Eight

On the Wisdom Road

Of life's many attractive options, I want to walk on the wisdom road,
for God's promises are many and they produce love, I'm told.
Of all the destinations, I want the one leading to more love as I get old.

Better than all the riches of life with jewels and fine silver,
will be my reserved seat at the Lamb's marriage dinner.

But as a man hunting for answers, I seem to have limited vision.
Only when I ask my Lord above, do I get the clarity of true wisdom.

Without which I would be lost and in a constant mess,
For my thinking gets corrupted, I must confess.

God wants to direct my paths, informing me which way to go,
But unless I bow my head and seek his will, I will never know.

And along the way, my blindness often leaves relationship damage,
making my own self-centered decisions leaves hurt and carnage.

Please Lord, love and forgive me and heal all the messes I've made.
Looking back, I can see that it's in my ignorance that your wisdom was betrayed.

I thirst for your wisdom to see everything as you see it,
and notice all the opportunities that your love, I can transmit.

For the sake of others, make me wise so they can experience you in me.
and everybody that crosses my path, your beauty and love they will see.

Winning the Final Battle for Your Soul before It's Fought

My Journal for My Journey

The way I would describe my wisdom growth rate is . . .

The way I would describe the difference between enfeeblement and empowerment in my life is . . .

The places in my life where I need more wisdom are . . .

I believe God wants me to think and pray about these heartfelt concepts discussed in this section . . .

One Final but Essential Thought

THIS BOOK HAS BEEN completely dedicated to assisting you in having a joyful journey from birth to death and beyond. But to be successful in making that happen, you must be willing to humbly confess that it is beyond your individual and human ability to ensure your journey's success. Behind everything that has been taught in this book there is one guiding principle that will ensure that you can and will have a successful journey along with a wonderful and awesome conclusion to the earthly part of your journey. But this will only be true if you do this one thing. But before we get to that one essential, guiding principle, allow me to tell you a true story that depicts exactly how it works.

I'm an avid dog lover. I have two Labrador retrievers. One is black and called Hope, and the other one is yellow, called Faith. Every day that I'm not traveling, we go for a walk in the woods, their favorite thing to do. Hope and Faith do not need a leash because they never allow themselves to get out of eyesight of me. I don't need to watch them, they watch me. Often, I'm on a horse, and I can go anywhere at any speed, and they will follow, never once allowing me to get out of their view. When we arrive back at the barn and I slide down off my horse, both dogs immediately come running and jumping up on me as if to say, "That was a lot of fun, Dad, and it's good to be home with you now." What both Faith and Hope do illustrates this truth far better than anything I could ever say. Here is the biblical foundational truth for the principle to which I'm referring, found in these six separate passages in the Bible.

> *So be strong and courageous! Do not be afraid and do not panic before them. For the LORD your God will personally go ahead of you. He will neither fail you nor abandon you.* (Deut 31:6, (NLT)

Life's Joy Killers and Joy Makers

> *The LORD your God who goes before you will himself fight for you.* (Deut 1:30a, ESVUK)

> *It is the LORD who goes before you. He will be with you; he will not leave you or forsake you. Do not fear or be dismayed.* (Deut 31:8, NIV)

> *For the LORD will go before you, And the God of Israel will be your rear guard.* (Isa 52:12b, NIV)

> *I will go before you and will level the mountains; I will break down gates of bronze and cut through bars of iron.* (Isa 45:2, NIV)

> *I will go before you and make the crooked places straight.* (Isa 45:2a, NKJV).

> *Plead my cause, O LORD, with those who strive with me; fight against those who fight against me.* (Ps 35:1, NKJV)

Most of the time we (and preachers and commentators) do not distinguish between God being with us and God going before us. Of course, I love the companionship of God being with me, but that is not the point I'm asking you to consider in order to have a successful and joyful journey. I want you to specifically think about God going before you. These are two very different sets of promises and responsibilities.

First, Let's take the obvious benefit of God always being ahead of us one moment or more in time and place. As my head is still on my pillow, my Lord is already into my next day. As I'm working for my family's needs now, God is battling things out in my behalf in my future. As I'm apprehensive about my imminent meeting with my doctor to get my biopsy results, God has already seen the report. Yes, God is in my now, but God is also in and managing my next challenge in my future. And what is he doing there? According to those Scriptures you just read, God clears the way for you by leveling the ground, fights your battles, removes difficult barriers, and straightens your crooked paths. All of these are tremendous promises and they are much needed. In a nutshell, it allows you to worry less! And that is really a big deal. But all these wonderful things are true only if we are following him who is out ahead of us. That is the one conditional thing that allows us to have the joyful journey to which this book is dedicated.

When my dogs and I are out going through the woods, they look up every few seconds to make sure they can still see me. If for some reason I have somehow escaped their vision, they immediately go into full panic mode, scurrying about until they reestablish visual connection with me.

One Final but Essential Thought

One of my dogs will immediately begin barking to sound an alarm if she loses sight of me. And this is what I want us to talk about. My dogs have accepted the responsibility to stay with me at all times.

So that begs the question, are you staying with and right behind God's leading? Are you constantly looking up to stay visually connected to him who is before you? Are you able to see him and that one-of-a-kind look that says, this way my child? Are you a constant Christ-follower? Is he guiding you through your life, through your day, in the decisions you are making, and in the activities in which you are engaged? Can you both see and hear God in your life, right now? When I'm out with my dogs and on horseback and about to make a sharp turn, I holler out, "This way girls." Immediately, at the sound of my voice, they change their routes, so we are always together going in the same direction at the same speed.

I confess, I used to read the Bible many times out of guilt. Isn't that what a good Christian should do? Thank God, it's different for me now. I'm ecstatic to share that I now read it for entirely different reasons. You see, I'm in love with Jesus, and I cannot get enough of him, and I love hearing him talk to me through his Word. I want to stay right with him every moment of every day. If I lose contact, I immediately go into panic mode and I fall into danger and confusion, and Satan has a heyday with the thoughts that come into my mind. That takes me down a death spiral where things go from bad to worse. I'm sure that's why verses like this are in the Bible:

> *Examine yourselves, to see whether you are in the faith. Test yourselves.* (2 Cor 13:5a, ESV)

When I'm out with my dogs, every few seconds they look up to know if they can still see me. That is my final thought in this book. Do as this verse says to have a joyful journey; test yourself by looking up every little bit to see if you can still see and hear Jesus. If so, you are in the right place and on the right road to have an abundant, joy filled journey! Godspeed!

Epilogue

How and Why This Book Happened
You Are the Central Reason

MAY I TELL YOU something personal? I think you will enjoy it because it ends up being all about you! It all started when I adopted an initial life verse over 40 years ago. I thought of it nearly every day. It was emblazoned on my heart, but its work was completed two years ago. My life verse was Psalm 37:4:

> *Delight yourself in the LORD, and he will give you the desires of your heart.* (ESV)

I loved this promise and quoted it to myself thousands of times. I believed it with every fiber of my being, and two years ago, it culminated in my life by causing me to write a book (*Untangling the Seven Desires of Your Heart*). That book allowed me to put into print all the heart secrets God allowed me to discover that made me love him for evermore. Understanding and fulfilling those seven desires of my heart that he had put there became my personal journey to emotional freedom, the ultimate emotional jailbreak.

After that book was published, it was time to turn the page and focus on a new life verse. My first verse had done its work in me. This new life verse would capture my heart in a completely different manner. My first life verse taught me all about my heart's insatiable love for Jesus; my new and current life verse compelled me to get out on the battlefield to defend the reputation of Jesus, by whom I am privileged to be loved. I strongly felt the need to focus on doing one thing for Jesus that he wanted me to do by using

How and Why This Book Happened

the gifts that he had given me. Here is how it all came together and how you came into the picture. First, here is my new life verse that is now infusing tons of energy into what I'm doing.

> *In their case the god of this world has blinded the minds of the unbelievers, to keep them from seeing the light of the gospel of the glory of Christ, who is the image of God.* (2 Cor 4:4, ESV)

Look closely at the verse and note that Satan is hellbent to blind everybody on planet earth from seeing the glory of Jesus, the one with whom I'm head over heels in love. I hate what he is doing to my Jesus, my Lord and Savior. And I hate how he is keeping people from seeing and falling in love with the one person who can do for them what nobody else can or will. But how do I unblind people so they see the glory of Jesus so they can begin loving him as do I? That's when it happened, and it all came together—in you! You are the key for that happening, not me! Please follow my logic. If they see that you are someone very different and endearing, someone so very unusual about you, so much so that they are prompted to ask that you what makes you so joyful, so very filled with hope, and you say, "It is because of Jesus," instantly the blindness caused by Satan will have been defeated, and that person will see Jesus in all of his radiant glory in a person. If that person is you, they will have an up-close view of Jesus, all because of who you are in Jesus! It's the joy emanating from the hope you have found in Jesus that cannot be hidden, it cannot be duplicated, it cannot be removed by Satan, and it cannot be counterfeited. You become the authentic work and showcase of Jesus Christ!

That is exactly how God wants it to work. Here is how he describes it, and you.

> *But in your hearts honor Christ the Lord as holy, always being prepared to make a defense to anyone who asks you for a reason for the hope that is in you; yet do it with gentleness and respect.* (1 Pet 3:15, (ESV)

Now do you see it? I am committed to doing everything I can to assist you in experiencing the joy Jesus wants to provide in you. He speaks of it in John 15:11.

> *"These things I have spoken to you, that my joy may be in you, and that your joy may be full."* (ESV)

Life's Joy Killers and Joy Makers

That is how this book came into being. It is dedicated to giving you biblical truths about joy killers and joy makers. And where, you ask, do you fit in to all of this? That is the very best part, you are a direct answer to prayer where God was asked to bring people like you and this book together so that that your joy can be made fuller. My congratulations to you for making yourself so available to God and following his prompting guidance to read a book like this. You are a direct and treasured answer to prayers! Please, enjoy Jesus and all the joy he wants to provide you! It will make you a poster child for Christ. And your joyful life will become more influential than a thousand words or a hundred sermons.

In his mighty love and grip,

LaVon

Additional materials supporting LaVon's book, Life's Joy Killers and Joy Makers along with his first book, Untangling the Seven Desires of Your Heart can be found and obtained by visiting his website at:

lavoninspirations.org

www.ingramcontent.com/pod-product-compliance
Lightning Source LLC
Chambersburg PA
CBHW071433160426
43195CB00013B/1881